Call to Selma

Call to Selma

Eighteen Days of Witness

Richard D. Leonard

Skinner House Books
Boston

Printed in Canada

Cover design by Suzanne Morgan
Text design by WordCrafters
Interior photos by Ivan Massar. Copyright © Ivan Massar.

ISBN 1-55896-421-5

Library of Congress Cataloging-in-Publication Data
Leonard, Richard D.
    Call to Selma : eighteen days of witness / Richard D. Leonard.
        p. cm.
    ISBN 1-55896-421-5 (alk. paper)
        1. Leonard, Richard D. 2. Civil rights workers—Alabama—Selma—Biography. 3. African Americans—Suffrage—Alabama—Selma—History—20th century. 4. African Americans—Civil rights—Alabama—Selma—History—20th century. 5. Selma (Ala.)—Race relations. 6. Selma-Montgomery Rights March, 1965. 7. Civil rights movements—Alabama—Selma—History—20th century. 8. Unitarian Universalists—New York (State)—New York—Biography. I. Title.

F334.S4 L46 2001
323.1'196073076145—dc21

                                                    2001048354

10 9 8 7 6 5 4 3 2 1
04 03 02 01

Note: First-hand accounts of the voting rights protests in Selma, Alabama, in 1965 frequently use the language in common use at that time to describe African Americans, i.e. "blacks" or "Negroes." We have chosen to leave this language unchanged for historical accuracy.

We have made every effort to include the names of all Unitarian Universalist ministers who participated in the voting rights demonstrations in Selma and Montgomery, Alabama, in 1965. If you have information about participants who have been omitted from the list on pages 147–148, please contact:
    Editor
    Skinner House Books
    Unitarian Universalist Association
    25 Beacon Street
    Boston, MA 02108.
We will make any necessary corrections in future printings of this book.

Contents

Introduction

March, 1965, Selma, Alabama—a time and place where violence and bloodshed horrified our nation, where justice won out over oppression, where love cast out fear, where hope proved justified.

Selma was a watershed event in our nation's history, perhaps the high point in our collective belief that we, together, could end racism and move ever closer to the ideal of the "beloved community." By 1965, that belief had already been sorely tested. President Kennedy had been assassinated and the resistance to dismantling America's version of apartheid had stiffened. Fault lines within the African American leadership were beginning to become visible as Black Empowerment began to move away from integration, toward separatism.

The story of Selma begins, not with triumph, but with tragedy and violence. After the passage of the Civil Rights Act in 1964, which banned segregation in public accommodations, America's black leadership identified the right to vote as the next great priority. A march was planned to begin on March 7, 1965, from Selma to Montgomery, Alabama's capital, to urge passage of the Voting Rights Act.

These are the facts:

Martin Luther King, Jr. and five hundred school children were arrested in Selma in February 1965. On February 18, a 26-year-old black man named Jimmy Lee Jackson was fatally shot by state troopers at a night march in Marion, Alabama.

On March 7, 1965, six hundred civil rights marchers left Selma, headed east on Route 80. The march ended after only six blocks at the Edmund Pettus Bridge, where state and local law enforcement officials attacked the marchers with billy clubs, hoses, and tear gas, driving the marchers back. The day became known as Bloody Sunday.

The following day, Martin Luther King, Jr., called on clergy of all faiths to join him in Selma.

On March 9, King led a symbolic march to the bridge, joined by 450 clergy. That night white demonstrators attacked Rev. James Reeb, a white Unitarian Universalist minister. Reeb died on March 11, and two days later the Unitarian Universalist Association Board of Trustees adjourned its Boston meeting and traveled to Selma to join the march.

The response built. King preached at Reeb's memorial service at Brown Chapel on March 15. President Lyndon Johnson called for passage of the Voting Rights Act and called out the National Guard to protect the Alabama marchers.

On March 21, 1965, more than three thousand marchers left Selma for Montgomery. Of the estimated five hundred white clergy now in Selma, over two hundred were Unitarian Universalist. On March 25, over 25,000 people joined the marchers at the entrance to Montgomery.

Five days later, on March 26, Viola Gregg Liuzzo, a Unitarian Universalist layperson from Detroit, was killed by the Klu Klux Klan as she was driving to Montgomery to pick up a carload of marchers.

That summer, on August 6, President Johnson signed the Voting Rights Act.

These are the facts. But what is their meaning?

At one level, Selma is the story of hope redeemed. The organizing efforts of the black leadership proved effective. Local black people were willing to risk danger to achieve their rights. White clergy, especially Unitarian Universalist clergy, stood in solidarity with African Americans. The power of the federal government was invoked in the cause of justice. The Voting Rights Act was passed within months and thousands of black candidates were elected to positions of political leadership in the South. Hope was redeemed.

But the cost was great—the cost in life, the cost in blood, and the cost to the American soul. Selma 1965 was one of the first times that live images of violence were sent into the living rooms of typical Americans. The images were not of some distant land, but of us. White America saw the reality of violence, which Black Americans had lived with for generations. Shock, disbelief, and anger provided President Johnson with the political support to move forward. Martyrs were created.

The fragile victory did not hold. As King took the civil rights struggle to Chicago and began speaking out against the Vietnam War and about issues of economic justice, the moral coalition that made possible the Voting Rights victory began to dissolve. The Vietnam conflict consumed Johnson and the nation. The Great Society programs languished, even those that had worked best. In 1968, King was assassinated. American cities went up in flames. Hope was replaced with fear.

We must remember that racism was at work even in the way the victory in Selma was achieved. The death of Jimmy Lee Jackson, a black man, did not receive widespread press attention. It did not result in hundreds of white clergy coming to stand in solidarity. It did not produce support from the federal government or the president. It took the death of James Reeb, a white man, to do that.

Selma was a watershed event no less in our own religious community than in the nation at large. The 1968 Cleveland General Assembly, in the face of demands by black Unitarian Universalists and their white allies, committed $1,000,000 toward black economic and community development. This commitment was abrogated two years later as finances became tight and the separatist demands of some black Unitarian Universalists came into conflict with long-held dreams of racial integration. During the 1970s and early 1980s, there was a widespread retreat from engagement with racial justice. Many persons of color, including myself, left Unitarian Universalism during this period.

Now, forty years later, the UUA's current commitment to transform itself into an anti-oppressive, antiracist, and multicultural faith offers a source of hope once again. After years of antiracism training, Unitarian Universalist congregations are making specific contributions.

In May, 2001, the First Unitarian Church in Wilmington, Delaware, sponsored a forum with all seven African American state judges, together for the first time, to expose racism in the criminal justice system. The judges, amid press coverage, called for a statewide review. The church, at the center of the effort, worked in partnership with Stand Up for What's Right and Just, a community-based group fighting racial profiling and mandatory minimum sentencing.

In June, 2001, the Cleveland General Assembly approved an Action of Immediate Witness calling for reparations to the survivors of the 1921 race riot in Tulsa, Oklahoma, in which white Unitarian leaders may have played a role.

In September, 2001, Arab children in Raleigh/Durham were harassed by whites in the aftermath of the attacks on the World Trade Center and the Pentagon. Unitarian Universalists, following an antiracism training program, decided to walk to school with those children to calm their fears.

For the past decade, Unitarian Universalism has been in the business of reclaiming the history of Selma. King's sermon at James Reeb's memorial service, lost for thirty-five years, has been found and published in the *UU World* magazine. On February 1, 2002, a memorial to the three martyrs of Selma (Jimmy Lee Jackson, James Reeb, and Viola Liuzzo) will be dedicated in the chapel of the Unitarian Universalist Association in Boston. The memorial will hold up the history of that time as proof that hope can be justified, bearing witness to the cost and serving as a testament to the hard struggle of ending racism.

The heart of *Call to Selma* is the story of one white Unitarian Universalist minister, Richard Leonard. It is a personal account, the diary that he kept of his own experiences and reactions as the story of Selma unfolded. It is therefore not "history," but personal reflection. It offers another window through which we can see these events. Leonard reports not only the marches and meetings, but also the experience of "cold feet," quite literally, on the final march to Montgomery, as well as his reaction to the death of James Reeb and his own luck in surviving while Reeb did not.

The excerpts from other Unitarian Universalists that follow Leonard's diary, also written by white participants, speak of foreboding and fear. They also speak of the spiritual support their commitment to being present provided them. These are the stories of white people only, and they cannot tell the full story of what happened. But they do give us the story of Unitarian Universalist involvement in Selma. They tell us why so many white Unitarian Universalists were willing to risk their lives to support their black fellow citizens' rights to equal treatment, and they tell us what they saw and felt and did there. These stories also offer witness to the courage and determination of the black leaders of the struggle.

I would like to express my deep gratitude to Dick Leonard for his willingness to share his personal journal of those days. And my personal thanks to Judith Frediani and Rev. Jack Mendelsohn, who collected the stories and reflections of other Unitarian Universalists who were present in Selma.

As the first black president of the UUA, I look both back and forward—back on our complex legacy of hopefulness, racism, and struggle; and forward to our ongoing work of transforming the faith we love and helping our world bend toward justice. This book is a source of hope for that important work.

Rev. William Sinkford
President, Unitarian Universalist Association

In the vicious maltreatment of defenseless citizens of Selma, where old women and young children were gassed and clubbed at random, we have witnessed an eruption of the disease of racism which seeks to destroy all America. No American is without responsibility. The people of Selma will struggle on for the soul of the nation but it is fitting that all Americans help to bear the burden. I call therefore on clergy of all faiths to join me in Selma.

— Rev. Martin Luther King Jr., telegram, March 8, 1965

At times history and fate meet at a single time in a single place to shape a turning point in man's unending search for freedom. So it was at Lexington and Concord. So it was a century ago at Appomattox. So it was last week in Selma, Alabama.

— President Lyndon B. Johnson,
address to joint session of Congress, March 15, 1965

The Journal

Rev. Richard Leonard traveled to Selma, Alabama, on March 8, 1965, as a minister of the Community Church of New York. Although he planned to remain only a few days, he quickly found himself immersed in the struggle there, finally walking the fifty miles from Selma to Montgomery. Throughout his stay in Alabama, he tried to keep detailed notes, sometimes on the backs of envelopes or on whatever pieces of paper he could find, often in the rain. On returning to New York City, Leonard dictated from his notes into a tape recorder to help organize his thoughts. The journal that follows is the result, only slightly revised in later years as some of his impressions were corrected by other participants.

Day One

Monday, March 8. I headed into our ministers' meeting at the Community Church of New York without the faintest idea that by nightfall I would be in the state of Alabama, and that for the next seventeen days I would be involved in an epic struggle that would fashion the future of our country, and to an extent, the world.

Donald Harrington, the senior minister of New York City's Community Church, his associate Rev. Melvin Van de Workeen, and I, the church's minister of education, had all witnessed on television the night before the beatings of the civil rights marchers in Selma, Alabama. We had heard Rev. Martin Luther King's appeal to clergy from all over the country to come to Selma to assist the protesters in their demand for voting rights.

I had long been active in the field of civil rights. As a student at the Union Theological Seminary in New York City in the early 1950s, I had helped "integrate" barber shops, under the auspices of the Congress on Racial Equality. In 1965 I was directing an interracial church school of three hundred children in the largest, and thoroughly integrated, Unitarian Universalist church in the country, the Community Church of New York.

Still, Alabama seemed a long way from New York. My responsibilities at the church looked heavy enough for the days ahead.

We talked. Don had been all over the country speaking for equality in race relations. Mel had been in Mississippi only recently, involved in lunchroom sit-ins. My only visit to the deep South had been as a teenager in a twelve-year-old car driving up through rural Texas and Arkansas. I remembered well the sign over the road in Greenville, Texas:

WELCOME TO GREENVILLE
The Blackest Dirt
The Whitest People

I had also attempted, with Donald Harrington, to attend the funeral for the four little girls killed in the Birmingham church bombing in 1963. On that occasion our planeload of civil rights

3

supporters had been turned back by a bomb threat. By the time the plane had been searched, it was no longer possible to make the connection in Atlanta that would get us to the funeral on time. So seventy northern sympathizers of the children and their families were effectively prevented from attending the funeral.

But now the arrow was swinging in my direction; indeed, it pointed straight at my heart. One of us was going to answer Dr. King's call. Fate had laid its warm hand squarely on my shoulder, and I said I would represent the Community Church.

I would go that afternoon. I would be back at my job in two or three days. Or so I thought.

The plane reservation was made for late afternoon. But there were logistical problems. One involved my beard. For two years I had been growing one, in the face of both jeers and compliments. Its main purpose was to remove the necessity of my having to shave twice a day. While beards were appearing more and more on the New York scene, I imagined that they would be nonexistent in Selma, and that I would be a natural target for a marksman, not to mention an embarrassment to the clean-shaven clergy I expected to meet there. The beard would have to come off before I left. I imagined I could take it off in ten minutes with scissors and a razor.

A much more delicate problem involved my relationship to my wife Barbara and my two daughters. Barbara, a psychotherapist, would, I thought, be lukewarm at best to the idea of hundreds of clergy converging on Selma, probably to get their heads knocked in the cause of civil rights. She would be unalterably opposed, I knew, to the father of our young children voluntarily risking life and limb in such a hostile atmosphere.

How would I tell her? Or should I even tell her before I reached Alabama?

It was already 2:00 p.m. The plane would leave Newark at 5:00 p.m. I had just enough time to pick up a few items at home and head for the airport.

At 2:30 p.m. when I reached home, Barbara was just heading out to meet her first patient of the day. To open a discussion of my plans at that moment would precipitate a first-class argument.

4

She would be unable to meet her patients, and I would miss the only flight that could get me to the march the following day.

I chose not to plunge into that bottomless pit. Rather, I would telephone her mother from the airport and have her break the news to Barbara, Suzy, and Elizabeth. I wondered what my children would think of their father.

Into a briefcase I quickly packed items that occurred to me: my black clerical robe so that I would look like a clergyman, a raincoat, several shirts, as much cash as I happened to have on hand, two pairs of socks (just right for a three-day expedition, I reasoned), aspirin, Band-Aids.

The removal of my beard proved a vast, unwelcome project. As much as I cut away, there always seemed to be so much more to come off. It was half an hour before I could even think of using a razor, and time was slipping away much too fast.

At last I could make the race by taxi to the airport. The plane was there, as were a few clergypeople whom I recognized, responding undoubtedly to Dr. King's call. I found Dwight Brown, the district executive of our Metropolitan New York Unitarian Universalist Association, and we happily agreed to share each other's company on the trip down.

Once airborne I began to take stock of the things I might have brought with me but didn't. I didn't have an umbrella or rain-shoes. Don had made a point of how much it rains in Alabama. My rainshoes were worn out at the heels and shipping water, and I had left them behind as useless.

I had no watch. The stem on my watch had inconveniently broken that very morning. Still, for a two- or three-day visit I thought it would scarcely be missed.

I had forgotten a toothbrush, anything resembling pajamas or extra underpants. One could manage for two or three days. Alas, the radio! I was used to carrying a small one on trips, just to feel linked to the outside world, but in my haste had forgotten to put it in my travel bag. (All of the aforementioned items were sorely missed in the 18 days that followed!)

As we tried to relax on the airplane and pretend that it wasn't going to be too dangerous a trip, things did not look too bad. The

stewardess came around taking orders for cocktails. I took toma-
to juice instead. A delicious dinner was served, and the stewardess went up and down the aisle pouring wine into empty
glasses. This I also passed up, thinking that I should probably be
in full command of my senses from that point on.

Before long we were in Atlanta. The airport looked like any of
scores that I have been in, except for the hangars labeled
Southern Airways. Moving into the terminal, however, we felt
the cool stare of employees and travelers, who seemed to sense
that we were not on a casual mission. How much of this coolness
was actually present, or only imagined because we expected to
find it, I cannot say. Still, it was nice to board another plane and
find it packed with clergy, all heading for Montgomery and,
eventually, Selma.

The second lap of our flight called for one brief stop en route,
in Columbus, Georgia, located on the border with Alabama. As
we took off again from Columbus into the night, I watched the
runway disappear beneath us. We moved over a large dark area
that might have been either a lake or a wooded area without
lights in it.

While we were still only several hundred feet in the air, I
looked further and saw a fire below us. It surprised me, since it
seemed to be in the middle of nowhere. As I watched it pass
below the plane, I was startled to realize that it had taken the
shape of a cross. I saw it for only a few seconds and then it had
passed behind us. Was I the victim of an overactive imagination?

I asked Dwight if he had seen it, but he had been looking in
another direction. To ask other passengers would risk being
dubbed paranoid or a "basket case" before we even landed in
Alabama.

But I resolved to speak to the pilot when we landed, to ask if
he had seen it also. Unfortunately, when we landed in Montgomery, there was no opportunity for me to talk to the pilot. I
suppose I will never know whether the Klansmen were out in
Columbus, Georgia, that night, warning the travelers to
Montgomery, or whether I only observed a brush fire that for the
moment assumed the shape of a flaming cross.

Needless to say, however, I took it as a warning and expected to see many more on my visit. It was the only one I saw.

Our arrival in Montgomery was uneventful, except that the coolness on the part of the employees at the Atlanta Airport turned in Montgomery to unmistakable iciness. We investigated the possibility of renting a car to get to Selma, but no cars were to be had, nor did anyone apparently want to speak to us. Already little groups of spectators were standing around the terminal looking at the rather large group of clergypersons, while we stood waiting uncomfortably for cars that had been promised to pick us up.

I was confronted with a new problem: what to do with an envelope containing almost $150 in cash. I had brought it with the thought that cash might be needed for bail money, or simply for subsistence. My plan had been to convert it into traveler's checks. But in the Montgomery airport at that hour no traveler's checks were to be had. I was reluctant to carry the envelope even in a car trip to Selma. So I placed it in a locker and carried only the key with me, again expecting to be back in several days to pick it up.

I had one more envelope to mail, addressed to my secretary in New York. It contained instructions regarding my memorial service in New York should I not happen to survive the next few days. While we all expected to be home by week's end, the closer we got to Selma, the more we realized that the entire venture could end in mayhem.

With that letter mailed, cars soon arrived from Selma, and some of us were on our way in a three-car convoy. The first two cars carried clergy. The third car contained Mrs. Paul Douglas, wife of the U.S. senator from Illinois; Mrs. Charles Tobey, widow of a former senator from New Hampshire; and Mrs. Harold Ickes, wife of the former secretary of the interior. We were gratified that people of such eminence, and women as well as men, were answering Dr. King's call.

Route 80 heading toward Selma seemed very dark and ominous. After a short distance we were stopped at a road-check set up by the State Police and the Department of Highways.

Apparently everyone going to Selma that night was being monitored by the police.

A young trooper came to our window, and while our car's license was being recorded, he shone his flashlight on us. He asked where we were from. We told him that we were from various cities. He asked if we were going to Selma on business, and we said we were. And with that he let us go. Apparently his instructions were to not engage us in discussion.

Our three-car convoy continued down the road into the dark of night, passing through Lowndes County. It could not have dawned on me that 18 days later I would be walking the same fifty-mile route, but in the opposite direction.

We were careful to observe the speed limit, remembering Andrew Goodman, James Chaney, and Michael Schwerner in Mississippi, whose eventual killing was precipitated first by a minor traffic incident.

An hour later we were entering the outskirts of Selma, crossing the Edmund Pettus Bridge, where the demonstrators had been beaten the previous day. We turned onto Selma's main street and were presented with a lovely, lamp-lit view. It could have been a town anywhere in the United States. For some reason I thought of Nebraska.

Then we made a turn toward the "Negro" area of the city and realized that the third car in our convoy was now a police car. What had happened to the car with Mrs. Douglas, Mrs. Tobey, and Mrs. Ickes? We did not see the three women again that night. I occasionally worried about them and was relieved when they turned up safely the next day.

Meanwhile the police car followed us a half-dozen blocks until we entered Sylvan Street, which runs in front of Brown Chapel.

Brown Chapel had for years been the focal point of the entire black community, and consequently became the headquarters for the resistance in Selma. It was 9:30 p.m. when Dwight and I emerged from our car and beheld an unbelievable scene.

Outside the chapel there was a sea of activity, with hundreds of people milling around and no place for arriving cars and buses. The picture inside the chapel was even more imposing. Every bit of floor and balcony space was occupied by a human being. The aisles were full, packed with people. The balconies looked as if they could collapse under their strain.

People sat in the windows. All of the vestibules and anterooms were tightly packed. For a long time we could not get into the main church sanctuary and could only strain to hear the speakers. But the singing, interspersed between the speeches, involved everybody and was close to deafening.

I could identify the voices of James Farmer of the Congress of Racial Equality (CORE), Ralph Abernathy of the Southern Christian Leadership Conference (SCLC), and finally Martin Luther King Jr. Others whom I could not identify were the local leaders of black Selma and the strategists of SCLC and the Student Nonviolent Coordinating Committee (SNCC).

All spoke eloquently on the meaning of the events of the previous day on the Edmund Pettus Bridge and the need for the people to act resolutely in the days ahead. Thunderous applause and cheers broke out with every exhortation. It was clear that tomorrow we would march several thousand strong along the same fateful route where the beatings had occurred Sunday. We would test the forces opposed to us, and our own will to prevail. Hopefully, we would march to Montgomery, though few of us had any idea how it would be done and in what amount of time.

At midnight the meeting broke up and I went to a designated place for lodging. My hostess was an aging but thoroughly delightful little woman who took four ministers into her place that night. I made a bed out of quilts on the floor and managed about five hours' sleep. Her place was on the edge of the Carver Housing Project, which abutted Brown Chapel. We were adjacent to railroad tracks. For several hours I was aware of trains passing through, their coupling and uncoupling, before they too became silent.

I had managed a telephone call from Atlanta to my mother-in-law, and by now my wife and daughters were aware of my whereabouts. Phones in Selma were too few and being used for high-level purposes. What was my family thinking?

Day Two

Tuesday, March 9. At 6:00 a.m. I was awakened by a rooster crowing, a strange sound in the ears of someone raised and living in cities. While others continued to sleep, I began organizing my thoughts around the fact that our stay in Selma might be longer than we had anticipated. I began to jot down notes of things I had already seen and heard and put them in chronological order.

Before long everybody was up. We were directed to the Greene Street Church for our breakfast. That church is also in Selma's black district, perhaps six blocks from Brown Chapel and the Carver Houses where most of the activity was occurring. Scores of volunteers from that community were cheerfully and quickly serving up a standard fare to several thousand people. I was amazed at the logistics of providing a single meal, much less that of accommodating several thousand visitors from distant places. Familiar faces were scattered in the crowd. A large number of beards on the men let me know that my struggle the day before to remove mine had been completely unnecessary and time wasting. Everyone in the church speculated about what might happen that day.

Returning to Brown Chapel, I found a seat before it filled to capacity, for a meeting that would determine whether or not we undertook the dangerous second march across the infamous bridge. This time I was writing feverishly on whatever paper I could find, in an effort to capture the spirit of the local people and the turmoil of the leadership.

Who was leading whom? I began to understand for the first time how militant the people were in desiring their right to vote and be treated with dignity, and at the same time how deeply committed most were to the philosophy of nonviolence.

One speaker noted that "if you took all the Negroes in Selma and combined their knowledge of explosives, you wouldn't be able to blow the clock off the back wall of the church." It was typical of the humor that was to surface at every meeting and worship service, which, along with the freedom songs, kept hearts high in the midst of enormous tension.

One after another of the speakers chided the leaders of the white community, from Governor George Wallace to Police Commissioner Al Lingo, to Sheriff Jim Clark, to Mayor Joe Smitherman and Public Safety Commissioner Wilson Baker. Sheriff Clark was clearly the greatest symbol of injustice and brutality. It was Jim Clark's deputies, or "posse" as they were known, who could be counted on to be violent. Clark had personally beaten a black woman and, when later asked by the press whether the woman was Miss or Mrs., replied, "She was a nigger woman; they ain't either Miss or Mrs."

A speaker said, "Jim Clark had better have his fun now, because he won't be around much longer when we get the vote." Another told the audience that if they had been awake most of the night without adequate accommodations (many had slept in the church on hard benches or on the floor), "just remember that Jim Clark stays awake all night when we stay awake all night. And sometimes while we sleep, he stays awake."

Another speaker noted that Sunday's brutality on the bridge indicated that Governor Wallace had decided that "the price of freedom is going up," to which the speaker responded, "We will tell him that the price of killing niggers is going up." He closed with the poem "We're in the same boat, brother," which ends,

When you rock one end,
You're going to rock the other.

As this meeting of several thousand was in progress, there was a great deal of planning and strategizing going on behind the scenes.

Two days before, immediately following the beatings and the tear gas, SCLC had applied to U.S. District Judge Frank Johnson for relief from the brutality, and the right to peacefully protest and march on the streets of their state.

Early Tuesday morning they received, instead, an injunction from Judge Johnson forbidding them from marching across the bridge. A speaker noted bitterly that this was probably the first time an abused party had applied to a federal court for relief and instead was forbidden to carry out the behavior for which they had been abused.

Judge Johnson's ruling precipitated a tremendous amount of soul-searching by the SCLC leadership. Up until that point they had always obeyed federal mandates, the federal government being looked upon as a friend in grievances against the states. Now there were thousands of people ready to march to Montgomery to make their protest to Governor Wallace, and the federal court was saying "Wait!" Dr. King spent all Monday night and early Tuesday trying to talk Judge Johnson out of his decision, and failed. His top leadership was divided, and the young people of SNCC were urging that the march proceed. All shades of heated opinion were coming to the floor in Brown Chapel.

Mrs. Douglas was seated near me. I asked her if she would participate in the march in the face of the federal injunction. She was very much torn. She had come to Selma in complete sympathy with the voting rights movement. Now, as the wife of a U.S. senator, she felt she would have to get her husband's advice before she could march.

From 9:00 a.m. until almost 2:00 p.m. the issue was debated. A few got up to say that there were other things we could do and that we needed to keep the federal government on our side. One or two speakers, at the other end of the spectrum, urged giving up the attempt at nonviolence and marching regardless of the consequences to ourselves, since it appeared that that was the only course that would obtain basic rights.

A minister friend of mine was not sure that he could remain nonviolent if being beaten up. Someone advised him to talk directly with one of the SCLC leaders to see if he should excuse himself from the march.

It became apparent that the overwhelming majority of the people in the meeting favored proceeding with the march in spite of the injunction. Dr. King had come to the same opinion. In anguished tones he told the huge gathering that the blacks had come too far to be turned back now, even by a U.S. court. The die was cast. We began filing out of the church.

On the sidewalk we were advised to walk six abreast. At the head of the line was Dr. King, a number of black clergy, and as many white dignitaries as could be brought forward. The line, numbering close to three thousand, reached down the block and filled a playground area. Interspersed among the black young people, male and female, were priests, rabbis, and ministers, black and white, and what seemed a disproportionately large number of nuns in their habits. It was hard to imagine that they would be beaten or teargassed, and the sight of their cheerful faces gave courage to others.

At 3:00 p.m. the orderly procession began to move down Sylvan Street, then made a right turn toward the center of the city. The great number of marchers must have made a strong contrast to the 625 marchers of two days before. Several ambulances and their crews stood along the way. The atmosphere was somber, interrupted by occasional bursts of freedom songs, often led by teenagers, some with magnificent church-trained voices. Several children might have been as young as ten. We passed little knots of people, black and white, watching us perhaps as much out of curiosity as anything else, until we came to the main turn in town toward the bridge.

At that point a U.S. marshal confronted Dr. King and the procession stopped. The injunction was read. Most in the procession could not hear Dr. King's response nor that of the marshal, but the marshal stepped back and the march continued, with the bridge now directly ahead. To add to our foreboding, we found ourselves now the target of angry insults and obscenities from groups of whites on either side of the road.

As we drew closer and closer to the structure, it seemed to grow larger and larger. When we had passed over it the night before, it had seemed an insignificant part of the road. Now it loomed over us and high above the river that ran beneath it. We could only see to the midpoint of the bridge because of the slope of the bridge on each side. We had no idea what lay beyond.

Passing over the midpoint, however, each rank of marchers could suddenly see far ahead toward Montgomery. But between the march and the open road was a scene that could not but strike fear into the heart of every participant, from Dr. King down to the last ten-year old. The might of the state of Alabama was drawn up in full array against the beleaguered protesters.

About two hundred state policemen in their brilliant blue uniforms and helmets lined both sides of the road, shoulder to shoulder, for a distance of several hundred feet. Beyond them, and linking one side to the other, another rank was stationed across the highway completely blocking the line of march. Every policeman held his club with both hands parallel to the street, making a solid cordon of wooden clubs. We were being invited to march into a pocket in which we would be surrounded on at least three sides by overwhelming force. My knees turned to rubber at the awesome sight.

The location was only slightly beyond where the beatings had occurred two days before. We were not unmindful of the fact that since we were disobeying a federal injunction, the police might feel they had every right to use the power they held.

Dr. King and those in the front ranks led us without wavering into what felt like a steel trap, until they could proceed no further. An explosion of violence seemed but seconds away. I glanced at the policemen six feet from me, and they reflected the same tension felt by the marchers. Their clubs were held so tightly that their knuckles were white. Their faces were expressionless. We waited for the signal for them to attack us.

Instead, Dr. King and the police commander spoke loudly at each other, the latter having benefit of a bullhorn. Word came back to us that we would hold a prayer service on the spot, and we all knelt. Mrs. Paul Douglas, apparently with the blessing of her husband, was brought forward to the first rank, followed by a line of sisters from the Roman Catholic Church, and more priests, rabbis, and ministers. Several of the clergy led prayers over the hushed crowd. We stood and joined in singing "We Shall Overcome."

At that moment we were amazed to see the troopers who directly blocked the road swing to the side, leaving the road to Montgomery wide open to us. Everyone felt a few moments of indecision and apprehension. Was this a cynically inspired effort to isolate us even further, or to lay the onus on us for continuing to march in the face of a federal court order?

Dr. King responded by leading the first rank, and consequently all the other marchers, in a U-turn that took us back toward Brown Chapel. Even as he made the turn, a part of each of us wondered why we had not followed the script that we had set out for ourselves only an hour earlier. But there was also relief that the bloody confrontation had been avoided, at least for the time being. Moving close to the police, I saw that a few of them had taunting grins.

The scene in Brown Chapel was bedlam. There was even talk that Dr. King had made a tacit agreement with the police ahead of time that we would turn back when we reached a certain point. People spoke of betrayal. The strategy for the future looked cloudier than ever. There would be a mass meeting at 7:30 p.m. in the chapel to try to sort everything out.

At dinnertime I was invited to go with a group of a dozen white Unitarian Universalist ministers to eat in a black-owned restaurant, Walker's Cafe, in the spirit of our giving maximum support to the black community. I demurred. I felt that they were getting a late start and would probably get back to the chapel after the meeting began. My prime interest was in hearing the debate about today's and tomorrow's actions and getting as much of the discussion into my notes as I could. I ate a hasty bite of food at the main serving area in the Greene Street Church and took an early seat in Brown Chapel.

By 7:30 p.m. we were heavily into a discussion of the afternoon's events. Dr. King gave his reasoning behind his apparent turnaround. First, we were successfully communicating the problem of the South to the whole country, he said. All eyes were upon us, even in distant parts of the world. Second, there were certain minimal things that had to be achieved today. One was to go as far as the marchers had gone Sunday. In fact, we had gone a bit farther. More important, the number of clergy, particularly white clergy, was growing rapidly, and this was a protection for the demonstrators. It was showing the world that the state of Alabama would commit violence when only blacks were concerned, but that if blacks and whites were both involved, the state was less apt to use its heavy hand.

Dr. King declared that he understood how frustrated many of us were, that we had been "prepared to carry the cross, and felt rather that we had ended up carrying a toothpick." But, he said, "Every step in this movement has to be considered in terms of long-range possibilities."

He announced that while we numbered about three thousand strong at this point, planes and buses were loading up all over the country with many, many thousands more on their way. Suddenly the wisdom of our putting together all the force that we could muster began to make today's choice seem like the right one. Hearts were lifting.

He concluded that we would in fact march to Montgomery "no matter how long it takes us to get there." The cheers that greeted that statement have seldom if ever been heard in a house of worship.

Only one damper had fallen on the meeting. Midway through, an announcement was made from the pulpit that three Unitarian Universalist ministers had been brutally attacked coming out of Walker's Cafe by white men. James Reeb was seriously wounded and on his way to the hospital in Birmingham. I would soon find out that the other two were my friends Clark Olsen and Orloff Miller. Jim Reeb and I had met only casually in Selma. I saw myself as, only by the grace of the most casual decision, saved from being in the ambulance instead of James Reeb.

When the announcement had come of the attack on the ministers, a mighty groan had gone up from the assemblage. But the meeting continued. Some of us needed more details, but did not know where to go for them.

Meanwhile a great deal of sarcasm was expressed about President Johnson's role in the developing crisis. Rev. James Bevel, one of SCLC's leaders, was coming more and more to the front as both orator and strategist. He stressed that what the movement faced now was not a race problem but a political problem. From his vantage our government was willing to parachute troops to the Congo, where the United States had no sovereignty, to help some desperate people, but unwilling to parachute men into Selma to protect the rights of U.S. citizens. He observed that the colonists had stood strongly in 1776 for the right to participate in government, something many blacks "didn't think too highly of today," and he admonished the blacks in the audience to have the same regard for self-government that the revolutionaries had in the 18th century.

In a comical aside Bevel said, "President Johnson certainly has a race problem of his own—if his daughter married a Negro, he would commit suicide!"

Another speaker, just arrived from the disturbances in Birmingham, said that by being firm in their city they had gotten rid of Sheriff "Bull" Connor. "Now the people of Birmingham are coming to Selma to help you get rid of Jim Clark." And, "We filled the jails in Birmingham and now we'll help you fill your jails." Already one third of Selma's adult black population had been in jail.

The meeting over, we rushed to get details on the attack on our fellow clergyman. We learned from Rev. Homer Jack that indeed a dozen of our denomination's clergy had eaten in Walker's Cafe, that all but three had left a bit earlier than the others in order to try to get to the 7:30 p.m. meeting on time, that the three had been walking away from the restaurant when apparently two whites came up behind them. Trying not to look back, they did not see one of them swing a two-by-four piece of lumber, which glanced off two of them but hit Jim Reeb squarely on the back of his head. The whites then ran off.

Reeb complained of intense pain in his head, then went down and had not regained consciousness. An ambulance was summoned, and Homer had accompanied Reeb toward Birmingham, where it was judged the nearest hospital was located that could treat that serious a wound.

But the ambulance, a decrepit vehicle operating only in the black community, had broken down and had had to return to Selma. While it was in the service station being attended to, and while another ambulance was being summoned, groups of whites had gathered around the station and begun to ask questions. They had become quite hostile, even as a man lay dying in the vehicle.

Finally the other ambulance took Reeb and several of our clergypeople to Birmingham. The time that had been lost added to everyone's sense that Jim's survival was not likely.

At midnight I lay down in my makeshift bed of quilts and had a fitful sleep until 6:00 a.m., little realizing that those six hours would be more sleep than I would manage, in total, in the next three days.

Day Three

Wednesday, March 10. It was my father's birthday. While I gave a few thoughts to my parents in Detroit and how upset they would be by now knowing their son was demonstrating in Alabama, my more immediate thoughts were with my wife and daughters, with whom I had had no contact for almost two days. But the long lines at the few telephones had so far prevented me from calling New York.

By 9:00 a.m. Brown Chapel was overflowing again. Freedom songs and hymns united blacks and whites, young and old. A decision was slowly crystallizing that we would march again that day, this time to the courthouse ten blocks away, since we were forbidden by federal order to walk to Montgomery.

It was at this meeting that I heard about Public Safety Commissioner Wilson Baker's "doohickey." Sometime during the months before, when demonstrations in Selma were becoming more numerous, Wilson Baker had strode into Brown Chapel in the middle of a worship service and installed a microphone right on the pulpit. He referred to it as his "doohickey" and called everybody's attention to it. He said he was putting it there so that the police would know exactly what was going on in their community.

The blacks had left the "doohickey" there and continued to conduct all their meetings, their worship, and their strategizing in the open, knowing that everything was being listened to at the police headquarters. In fact, the "doohickey" was seen as an instrument for educating the police. Statements were made directly from the pulpit to the police department. Then one day, perhaps from outside pressure but more likely from realizing that he was being taunted, Wilson Baker came down the aisle with just as much bravado and removed his microphone.

The story fit neatly into our picture of how the police in Selma operated. We assumed that all telephone calls were being tapped. One newsman said that after he dictated a news story on the telephone, a voice completely unknown to him came in with "I got it." Other members of the community told of picking up their telephone and hearing a jangle of assorted noises and sounds at the other end that sounded very much like police headquarters, a location they were all becoming very acquainted with. Obviously a tap had been forgotten and the wire left open.

It seemed prudent to us visiting clergy that we should make all of our calls from the telephone in the parsonage at Brown Chapel. We assumed it was tapped and reminded each other not to discuss SCLC's evolving strategy. The penalty for limiting ourselves to one telephone was an interminable line.

As the 9:00 a.m. meeting progressed, there was more discussion regarding our turning around the day before. We learned that U.S. Attorney General Nicholas Katzenbach had pleaded with Dr. King not to make the march. So had Leroy Collins, a former governor of Florida, whom President Johnson had just appointed to be his personal representative in Selma in the deepening crisis.

Rev. Andrew Young spoke movingly. "We are tired of any Johnson, Lyndon or Frank, trying to use the legal machinery of the nation to manipulate Negroes and suppress their given rights." He noted that "the whole movement in Albany, Georgia, was killed by fooling around with a segregationist federal judge," and that "Moral issues come above legal ones. When the law is obviously unjust, a person has no recourse but to protest the law and act out of conscience." He drew howls of laughter when he concluded, "Mayor Joe Smitherman has asked us not to march. Joe Smitherman has never wanted the Negro to go anywhere at any time."

The decision was made that we would march peacefully to the courthouse to protest the attack on Jim Reeb and to present a number of statements on the courthouse steps from representatives of the various groups now present in Selma. It was thought that we should demonstrate our wide geographical background, and I agreed to make a statement on behalf of the participants from the state of New York.

While that march was shaping up, I managed to get to the parsonage telephone and place a call to my secretary at the Community Church in New York, Cynthia Jones. I asked her to cancel a number of appointments since I would be in Selma longer than I'd thought. And since we were each entitled to only one telephone call at a time, I asked her to call my family and reassure them that, despite what they were hearing about the attack on Jim Reeb, I was, and would continue to be, all right.

By 2:00 p.m. we had filed out of the church and lined up again, this time for the march to the courthouse. The number of clergypeople present seemed prodigious. A very long procession began its way along Sylvan Street toward the courthouse, again led by Dr. King and his associates.

But the police quickly formed ranks at the end of the block. Wilson Baker, alternatively with his arms crossed or talking through his bullhorn, announced that it was not conducive to our safety or to the safety of the people of Selma for us to continue.

After protestations from the marchers, Dr. King decided that we would deliver our message on the spot where we were being blocked. Many speakers came forward to speak for their groups. I tried to "speak for the state of New York" and the Unitarian Universalists as well, in a completely unprepared statement. We were aware of reporters from various newspapers, some of them liberal, some of them openly segregationist. I was unaware of any TV cameras present, and so was more than surprised several months later to learn that friends of ours, visiting England in March, had been amazed to see and hear me make that "speech" on TV there. Our message had gone a long way. My friends reported back that I had made the point of how hard it was for the blacks in Selma to keep adhering to the principle of nonviolence while they themselves were being violated.

Other speakers noted other things. One said, "I look out upon a sea of more than fifty policemen, deputies, and troopers, and I see only the flags of a foreign nation." He was referring to the fact that all the green helmets of the sheriff's deputies and all of the state police cars bore the flag of the Confederacy—there was not a single U.S. flag to be seen. (The next day when the green helmets showed up on the line again, all the Confederate flag decals had been removed.)

As each of us came to the microphone to speak, the official police photographer took our picture, and we became a part of the police files of Selma and the Alabama State Police.

The unending number of speeches was producing a kind of stalemate between police and demonstrators. Suddenly we were aware that something of significance was happening behind us.

To our surprise, indeed dismay, those of us at the "front" end of the line witnessed the "back" end of the line moving away from us. The younger people, representing to some extent the philosophy of SNCC, the Student Nonviolent Coordinating Committee, had become impatient with the march's failure to make progress toward the courthouse. Perhaps they were also impatient with the content of the speeches. They had done an about-face and were heading in the other direction on Sylvan Street.

They intended apparently to reach the courthouse by a different route, going around the police. It was a tense moment, because they risked confrontation with the police and the townspeople on less than equal terms, with a strong possibility of a riot resulting.

Many of the adults raced in full pursuit. At the end of the very long block there was a confrontation within our own ranks. While arguments raged there, other young people slipped through backyards and were pursued by concerned SCLC devotees. Many of those were turned around just before they were met by an equally frantic police force.

Gradually the police were able to regroup, this time forming a second cordon at the far end of Sylvan Street as well. Slowly everyone drifted back to the original line of confrontation almost in front of Brown Chapel.

Still, some would not abandon the idea of going to the courthouse in small, orderly, integrated groups. Handfuls of people were slipping away avoiding the police. It was a time of decision for the clergy, especially the white clergy. How involved did each of us want to be? Technically any group of five or fewer persons could walk along a sidewalk anywhere in Selma without breaking the law. If white priests and ministers did not go along, it seemed obvious that the more actively minded students would go anyway. Their having clergy along might help to defuse a situation, or if people were getting hurt, the clergy might again be of assistance.

On the other hand, the presence of white ministers accompanying black youths might itself be a spark that ignited the anger of irresponsible deputies or white townspeople. Each of us was making a deep personal decision as to our role in a crisis that was becoming more fluid all the time.

At this moment a young black man about twenty years old came up to me. Would I accompany him to a restaurant in the black community? He, incidentally, was a highly individualized person wearing a big bear hat and other items that would make him stand out in a group. He was also heavy. And he looked as though he could easily be violent under violent circumstances. I was not sure whether his word "restaurant" was a code word for "courthouse."

If I chose not to go with him, it would be apparent that I was more concerned for my own safety than anything else. (Already we were getting some mild complaints that some of the white folks just wanted to put in an appearance in Selma for the benefit they would get back home.)

I thought for several seconds about his invitation and agreed to accompany him. In my mind I would go with him to a restaurant, but try to talk him out of an attempt to get to the courthouse.

As we walked calmly past the police line I discovered that we were three, not two—another young black man had joined us. We were still within the boundaries of what was permissible. But a white person walking with two blacks on a Selma street would, under ordinary circumstances, raise eyebrows; that day it brought very hostile stares. I screwed up my courage and we walked on the sidewalk of one of Selma's main streets.

We approached an intersection where a policeman sat on his motorcycle talking to another man. The policeman was obviously there to control the situation. My new friend said in a lowered voice, "You see that man standing alongside of the policeman? Well, they're both watching us, and if that man comes over here and starts beating on us, the policeman is just going to sit there on his motorcycle. They are good friends, and the police will not come to your aid." I found his observation less than comforting.

The man and his police protector held their ground and we walked a few blocks farther, not leaving the black community but coming closer to the white one and, I judged, the courthouse.

Suddenly my escorts led me into a restaurant. We sat down to friendly stares from the black patrons and black employees. I thought it might even be the same restaurant where James Reeb had been bludgeoned the night before.

Menus were not immediately forthcoming. As we sat, and sat some more, I found my appetite and my courage both dwindling. I was the only white person in the restaurant. I had accompanied my new friends there, which is what I said I would do. Now it became clear what I had to do, in the name of my own sanity.

I apologized to them for not being hungry, and said something about having responsibilities elsewhere as well as there. Their smiles did not seem cynical but rather grateful that I had gone a few steps with them. I got up, walked out the door, and was almost surprised not to find someone there ready to swing a two-by-four.

Now I was alone. Very much alone. About as alone as I ever want to feel. A white person in the black community, but at least a half-mile from the warm confines of Brown Chapel.

I decided I would avoid the main streets on the way back, in favor of the shortcuts I had seen the young people take. I worked my way through unfamiliar backyards. Soon I realized that I was not as sure of my directions as I had thought I was.

As I came out of another backyard to a street, I found parked on the street about forty police cars. They were parked on both sides of the street, gleaming in the sun. Apparently most of the state troopers had parked their cars on that street while they deployed at opposite ends of Sylvan Street to contain the demonstrators.

I cut across the street, expecting a voice to call out, "Hey, you! What the hell do you think you're doing?" The voice never came. No policemen had stayed behind to guard their cars or take a nap. A few minutes later I was back on Sylvan Street.

Reflecting, I looked back on the restaurant episode as a serious mistake on my part, if I was interested in my own safety. But I had demonstrated to a small degree my willingness to "walk the walk."

Other ministers, priests, and nuns went with other groups that afternoon. Some made it to the courthouse. One group was surrounded at the courthouse by an angry crowd and subjected to angry threats. As predicted, the sheriff's "posse" had joined in the abuse rather than defend the protesters. That particular group was finally more or less escorted out of the larger crowd and walked back to Sylvan Street.

It was a day when tension was keen everywhere, and everyone knew that almost anything could happen. Clergy accompanying the small groups may have saved the day in keeping the peace, such as it was.

Back in the Carver Houses I felt exhausted by the tension and headed toward the room where I had been staying, intent on getting an hour or two of sleep on my makeshift bed. But as I drew near to my hostess's building on the edge of the project, I found a policeman in his bright blue car almost at her door. I dared not go farther, lest I endanger both her and myself.

Back in Brown Chapel I fortunately ran into my hostess and she cheerfully and easily transferred me to another home for bedding down, a home much closer to Brown Chapel and the activity around it. Meanwhile, my bag and my few personal items were back in my original lodging. The bag happened to be a very unusual shape, not something one of the project dwellers was likely to own. I had to leave it there as long as the police were posted outside her door.

In my new quarters I slept on the floor for perhaps an hour. About 6:00 p.m. I was awakened by a jingle on the radio advertising a "Lion's Club Outing." It was being repeated over and over again, and the final line was *"Everybody* is invited." What an irony, that "everybody" for the Lion's Club meant every *white* person! I tried to picture everybody, including the demonstrators, suddenly descending on their fish fry, or whatever the event was, and the three separate police forces racing around madly to "protect" the Lion's Club members.

At 6:30 that evening we were back in the chapel for another meeting. It was decided that we should attempt a peaceful march that evening to the courthouse solely to hold a vigil for James Reeb, who lay in a coma and probably dying in the Birmingham hospital.

We lined up on Sylvan Street six abreast and again marched toward the courthouse. And once more, as we got to the end of the block, we were met by about 150 policemen. In the front rank were the city police in their white helmets, behind them the sheriff's deputies in their green helmets, and then the state troopers in their blue ones. The blue helmets were the most numerous and looked like the ocean behind the others.

Commissioner Baker told us that we could not march. We said that we would hold our vigil for Rev. Reeb right on the spot where we were being stopped, and the vigil began. Prayers, songs, and speeches were interspersed with periods of silence as we stood almost nose to nose with the police line.

The vigil went on and on. It was a clear night. Just about everybody who had marched at all that day, hundreds strong, stood facing the police six abreast. The police stood with the same stoic resolution. One o'clock became two o'clock, then three, then four. Again and again young voices and mature ones joined in singing songs with words like "Ain't gonna let nobody turn me 'round, turn me 'round, turn me 'round; Ain't gonna let nobody turn me 'round, in Selma, Alabama." And thus began the real stalemate that was to continue day and night for a number of days.

We took turns coming up to the front line to speak and sing and stand within inches of the police. Women and young people came out of the church to bring us coffee periodically, and sandwiches. Some demonstrators, wearying, went off to get their sleeping bags and returned; some simply lay down on the street. Many, however, stood all night, or took at most a few hours off to sleep in the pews of Brown Chapel. Some of the leaders sat in chairs just facing the police.

As the night wore on, we were gradually becoming aware that, just standing there, we were standing for something. It was an exhilarating feeling. The exhaustion I had felt in the afternoon, eased by one hour's sleep, had given way to a buoyancy that would not let me sleep. I knew then that it would carry me on a wave all the way to Montgomery.

When the time came.

Day Four

Thursday, March 11. By 9:00 a.m. everybody who had left the line for short periods during the night, or for a quick breakfast in one of the churches, was back in place, ready to march. We numbered in the hundreds, perhaps a thousand.

Public Safety Commissioner Wilson Baker was asked to let the march to the courthouse proceed, that we might hold a prayer vigil there for the stricken Jim Reeb. Permission was again denied.

The commissioner emphasized his decision by personally stringing a clothesline across Sylvan Street at the point where opposing forces met. He tied the rope to a telephone pole on one side of the street and to a metal pole on the other. He himself retired, probably to get some much-needed sleep. But the phalanx of police, shoulder to shoulder and several deep, with others in reserve, left no question about their resolve to contain us. We left no doubt about our resolve to go ahead by again coming up almost nose to nose with the police along the full length of the rope.

Dr. King and Ralph Abernathy of the SCLC were not present for this, having been served papers to testify in court that day. They had been whisked away at 6:00 a.m.

We stood behind the rope as hour after hour passed that day, singing songs and offering prayers for Jim Reeb and for Jimmy Lee Jackson, the young black man who had been shot by police in Marion, north of Selma, during a demonstration there. He had died of his wounds on February 25 in the Selma hospital.

Prayers were given for Governor George Wallace, that he might have a change of heart and himself be freed from the oppression of racism, and for the state troopers opposite us, forced by the situation to also hear our prayers.

Meanwhile, meetings went on almost continuously in Brown Chapel. People would take turns attending the meetings to find out what was going on, and then returning to the line.

By 4:00 p.m. the younger blacks and a few whites were so restless to move that I was afraid they might swarm around the line and precipitate an incident if not a riot. It took a number of us continually talking to them to hold them back. They knew the dangers of proceeding against police orders, but were coming to the conviction that the only way to make the country fully aware of the degree of oppression in Alabama was to offer up their bodies as a witness to their faith.

The songs continued, always spirited, always including the love they felt for everybody, and their desire to be free.

At 8:00 p.m. word came that Jim Reeb had died in the Birmingham hospital. Wilson Baker was reliably reported to have asked the SCLC leadership if the demonstrators "could control their own people" when they got the news. He was told that there would be no problem on our side of the line—we wondered if he and Sheriff Clark could control their men.

At the announcement of Jim Reeb's death, everyone on our side of the line knelt, and a worship service was put together

27

remembering him and his family, and those who encouraged and participated in the kind of brutality that killed him.

Darkness fell. Several hundred at the line continued their songs and began taunting the police more sharply. One song went, "I love everybody, I love everybody, I love everybody in my heart" (repeated). In succeeding verses they would name everybody. "I love Governor Wallace, I love Governor Wallace" and "He can't make me doubt it, he can't make me doubt it" and "I know too much about him, I know too much about him."

Then it would be, "I love Wilson Baker," and "I love Chief Al Lingo," and "I love Martin King," and "I love old Bull Connor," and "I love Jimmy Jackson," and "I love Lyndon Johnson," and "I love all the troopers," and on and on into the night.

There were also gentle taunts of the police, calculated not to inflame but to keep them aware of our feelings. They would scornfully call the police our "baby sitters," or call them "Lingo's kids." One person said into the microphone, "The only way you can keep us in the streets is to be in the streets yourself."

Sometime that night four of us came up spontaneously with a new song to help fill the time, "The Berlin Wall." To the tune of "Joshua Fit the Battle of Jericho," it went "We've got a rope that's a Berlin Wall, Berlin Wall, Berlin Wall. We've got a rope that's a Berlin Wall, in Selma, Alabama." It was picked up immediately by all the protesters and sung loudly into the night and at the police.

We began cranking out verses like a spigot that had been turned on. "Hate is the thing that built that wall, built that wall" and "Love is the thing that'll make it fall, make it fall" and "We're gonna stand here 'til it falls, 'til it falls." More verses were added as days passed, and the song became Selma's dubious contribution to the folk music of our country.

The "Selma Wall" for a few days was symbolic of the underlying grim determination of civil rights advocates to overturn patterns in the South that had openly been discriminatory. It was also a symbol of how inflexible others were to maintain the status quo. Newsmen and photographers flocked to the Selma Wall at all hours of the day and night to show the world something that had become a standoff, with worldwide interest and implications.

Occasionally there was an event that reminded us that, although we had not bargained for it, we were involved in life and death matters. Even as we sang, a young man many ranks behind me was hit in the head by an object, though not seriously hurt. A search revealed the object to be a small steel ball, "such as might have been used in the Civil War," someone guessed. It had not been fired from a gun, but probably been launched from a slingshot. It appeared to have come from the parked police cars or beyond them.

About a half-hour later a young teenage black girl was hit in the mouth with another steel ball, this one puncturing her lips and loosening several of her teeth. I happened to see her bloody face before she was taken for emergency dental work.

Very soon after, Governor Collins, President Johnson's representative, appeared on the scene. His first question was addressed to the state police. "Where are those pellets coming from?" There were no more pellets that night.

Shortly after supper it started to rain. I was to discover that when it rains in Alabama in March, as Donald Harrington had warned, it can look like Burma during a monsoon. The first thought was to give some protection to the people standing at the line.

As the rain dramatically increased, a large tent appeared out of nowhere and was hastily assembled. But Wilson Baker announced that he could not permit a tent to be placed on the street because it might be a "fire hazard." It was moved to the sidewalk, leaving those facing the clothesline exposed to the rain while the police moved judiciously into their cars.

Large plastic sheets were brought out of nowhere along with nondescript pieces of material. People held them over as many heads as would fit under each piece. One person's "runoff" was another person's "drenching." Yet nobody seemed to be irritated by others' miscalculations. The sounds of laughter and pouring rain were remarkably blended.

But arms grew weary holding up plastic sheets filling with water. New means of support were needed, and they appeared in the form of sticks, broom handles, metal pipes, anything that was reasonably straight and able somehow to be anchored.

Eventually something like thirty props were holding up an improvised tent, under which perhaps fifty people huddled. The structure that was immediately facing the police was so precarious and dilapidated that it became the butt of endless jokes on the part of the protesters. Someone suggested that after we marched to Montgomery, we might leave the shelter as a permanent monument to the civil rights cause. Another predicted that when the sun came up and the police awoke in their heated and comfortable cars, the very sight of our make-do shelter would cause them to flee in all directions.

Around midnight I slipped away to Brown Chapel to sleep on the floor, with my clergy robe as a pillow. About 2:00 a.m. I was wide awake again and certain that I needed to be back on the line to help maintain morale in the continuing rain.

As I had guessed, our ranks had diminished considerably in the adverse weather, to somewhat fewer than fifty bodies. All of the police rested in their cars, most undoubtedly sleeping, secure in their belief that nothing could possibly happen in the middle of a rainy night.

About 4:00 a.m., eight young people came out of the chapel, walked to a point just behind the last protester and stationed themselves at equal distance from one another facing the opposite end of Sylvan Street. Something was in the wind.

The people on the line looked over their shoulders and saw a group ready to march in the opposite direction, and they began to drift away from the line, to fall in behind new leaders. Without knowing why, those of us at the "front" of the line did an about-face, and the whole group was now ready to march away from Wilson Baker's clothesline.

Off the group went. One policeman must have opened his eyes at that moment to a very unexpected sight. The entire body of demonstrators was marching away from him in the rain at 4 o'clock in the morning.

Car doors slammed. Shouts rang out. Messages were being given into radios. Newsmen jumped out of their cars, clutching their cameras tightly and trying not to end in a heap in a puddle of water. Car engines revved up and cars began to move out.

"To the rear, march!" came a command from an unknown leader. In almost military precision the little group of marchers turned in their tracks and stepped smartly back to the clothesline, to the astonished stare of many law enforcers and newspeople.

We were quite sure that Wilson Baker had been roused from his sleep, wherever he was at that moment. We had let the police know that we were serious in our goals, and that we did not appreciate them sleeping in their cars while we stood in the rain.

There were other incidents that night, both comical and portentous. High spirits prevailed. As we stood at the clothesline, a hand came reaching through with a big pair of scissors, as if to cut Wilson Baker's line in two and open the route for the marchers. Just as quickly, the hand with the scissors was yanked back into the crowd by someone else's hand.

Someone suggested that the whole group assemble at the other end of Sylvan Street and then have a foot race past Brown Chapel toward the police, to see who could actually be the one to break the clothesline in the race to the courthouse.

At 5:00 a.m. I still counted fifty people standing at the Selma Wall, opposed by forty police cars, each with probably several men in it. This overabundance of force to contain an essentially peaceful demonstration was marking our entire visit to Selma. And behind our line of confrontation, our black hosts and hostesses were most generous with their very limited means, bringing sandwiches and coffee, blankets, and for me, an umbrella.

A very young boy had pressed a dainty gray woman's umbrella into my hand early in the evening. I saw the owner of the umbrella, a middle-aged woman, standing on the sidelines, herself now in the rain without an umbrella. I refused it. The boy insisted, and she nodded. I said to him, "All right, I'll take the umbrella, but on one condition, that you come back later and claim it." He nodded as though he understood.

He did not come back for it that night, nor in the days ahead. I carried it continually after that, hardly using it at all because of the ridiculous figure I thought a 6'3" clergyman would make with a woman's umbrella, and the fact that almost no one else had one. Why shouldn't I be as soaked as everyone else?

I also remembered wryly that Mohandas Gandhi, the exponent in India of nonviolence and a hero at my Community Church in New York, had carried little more than his eyeglasses, a parasol, and a watch. I lacked now only the watch. The parasol went all the way to Montgomery, then on the plane with me to New York, and thirty six years later is one of my most treasured possessions.

Day Five

Friday, March 12. Early the next morning word came to us that we would be permitted to march to the courthouse that day. It seemed like a big victory, possibly presaging a march to Montgomery. We would leave Brown Chapel at 10:00 a.m.

When 10:00 came, Wilson Baker announced that he had been overruled—there would be no march today.

The on-again, off-again decision created the greatest frustration we had yet felt. Some advocated charging through the rope, past the police, for the courthouse. But cooler heads prevailed. Debates raged within Brown Chapel, as speakers from SCLC and SNCC offered conflicting proposals.

While we were meeting in the chapel in the early afternoon, and while a relatively few stood opposite the police, Wilson Baker strode from his car to the line and, in a grand gesture, snipped the rope neatly with a big pair of cutters. Was this a message? Were we free to march? Or was this a cynical come-on, daring us to try to pass through the police at our great peril?

Explaining his action, Baker said that he had originally put up the rope for our protection and convenience, to help us maintain discipline. Since we didn't want it, he was taking it down. He guessed out loud that it would be harder for us to control our group without the clothesline.

Indeed, it was. Without the physical rope to hold us in, it was very difficult to keep people from surging down the road.

However, in our meetings within the chapel, it was stressed over and over and yet again that we must all move together, according to plans worked out by the leaders of the movement. To fragment was to play into the hands of the oppressors and invite their overwhelming use of force. One speaker (James Bevel, I believe, who was doing the best job of keeping SNCC and SCLC communicating with each other) said, "I'm not going to cross that line just to please Wilson Baker. By staying until the right moment, we can wreck Wilson Baker's mind." Discipline was winning out, over spontaneity and self-sacrifice and foolishness.

Meanwhile, the police looked no less menacing blocking our path—the only difference was that the rope was gone, cut up into pieces by the protesters and passed around as souvenirs.

One policeman had developed an obvious fixation on me. Several times he caught my eye, tapped his nightstick in his hand, pointed it at me, and nodded. I hoped that we would never meet if and when all hell broke loose.

One of the sheriff's deputies appeared on the line with a billy club about five inches thick at its business end. It was an awesome weapon, held by a pimply-faced kid not older than twenty, a "volunteer" in the emergency, and a walking picture of ignorance and brutality. The only time in eighteen days that I saw state troopers laugh was at this raw member of the sheriff's "posse," with his enormous club.

We tried singing "The Star Spangled Banner" once, to indicate our patriotism toward our country. It was, of course, too much to expect the police to remove their helmets. Our "raw recruit" used the opportunity of hearing the national anthem to spit on the ground as vigorously as he could.

As the day wore on, my lack of sleep began to catch up with me. I later calculated that in a sixty-six-hour period I had had only three hours of good sleep. Just as disconcerting as the fatigue was the absence of my watch, broken the day I left for Selma. I looked at my wrist, without its watch, hundreds of times in eighteen days. Though others had watches, and there was always the clock on the wall of Brown Chapel to refer to, I cared less and less what time it was. Once, when I asked a small girl whether it was morning or afternoon, she recoiled in absolute fear, as if I was insane. My deteriorating appearance did not help.

The fatigue factor had a peculiar manifestation. As the hours went by, it was simply impossible to feel more tired. I knew I was becoming somewhat irrational. I made the discovery that I could always rest one part of my body, my mind or my limbs, while making the other part work. But I dared not let them both sleep at the same time.

For example, if I had to walk between two points, even a block apart, for a meal or some decision-making meeting, I would let my mind sleep totally while I walked. Not a thought went through it. Then in the meeting, while my mind worked, I could let my body fall into a complete physical rest where there was not the slightest impulse to move a single muscle. It was an experience that I imagine every combat soldier must know intimately, when to fall completely asleep might mean being killed.

At any point I could have found a bed in the home of my second hostess. But during these first five days in Selma, every moment seemed crucial to the total event. One did not want to wake up in a comfortable bed in the midst of mass killings. The thought of riot, particularly led by the sheriff's deputies and the likes of Reeb's attackers, was never far from anyone's mind.

One of our Unitarian Universalist ministers, Ken Marshall, told a small group of our denomination's clergy that he was sure that every one of us had already single-handedly prevented a riot on more than one occasion. It was a believable statement.

That afternoon, with the rope down, the demonstrators began to move back and forth on Sylvan Street. They would march up to the police line, then turn and run in the other direction, necessitating a police presence at the end of the block, then race back to the original line, in a war of nerves that was bound to wear someone out.

There was also talk of serious dissension between SNCC and SCLC. I gradually learned that there was much less disagree-

34

ment than the press was trying to play up. Everyone knew that SNCC had been hard at work on voter registration in Selma and elsewhere for several years, and that SCLC was in Selma because SNCC had invited Martin Luther King and his associates in. But SCLC gave the movement a world-respected voice that SNCC otherwise lacked. Each group knew it leaned heavily on, and its survival might even depend on, the other.

An example of that interplay occurred as we sat in the chapel that afternoon. One speaker gave the strongest appeal yet for everyone marching, then and there, out of the chapel, through the police presence, and on to the courthouse. The crowd gave him a thunderous ovation, and some were rising to their feet to go.

An SCLC leader came over to the speaker, whispered a few words in his ear, and the speaker turned back with a sheepish grin and said, "Well, maybe we won't do it that way."

Still, the restlessness was growing in all of us as hours were turning into days and we were not permitted even an orderly march to the courthouse a mile away, much less to Montgomery fifty miles away, the ultimate purpose of our coming together and the indelible promise made by Dr. King.

Given that restlessness, I was immediately apprehensive early that evening when the rumor began to go around that "all of the clergy" were being invited to go to a meeting outside the area of the Carver Houses altogether. I simply could not picture taking all the clergy, black and white, which meant 98 percent of the movement's adult leadership, off the scene altogether.

It seemed official. Presidential Representative Leroy Collins was going to have a meeting with all of the clergy, somewhere off the site. In my tired mind I was able to conceive that a gigantic plot was underway, from Governor Wallace down to Sheriff Clark, to take the leadership out of the project, capitalize on the emotions of those left behind, and start the riot that would put the entire black community at the mercy of the police and local townspeople, thus ending what had become an intolerable stalemate for the state of Alabama. By and large, the whites would be spared, and the blacks, in the eyes of the conspirators, would get what was coming to them for focusing world attention on their town.

I tried to find out where the announcement of the meeting had come from, and traced it to a telephone call to the parsonage. Furthermore, the place of the meeting had been moved at least once. It would now be at the Roman Catholic rectory, said to be about ten blocks away. Governor Collins would meet with the "out-of-state" clergy.

By now I was aware that Dr. King and many of his associates were, by chance, also away from the Carver Houses. The white clergy were being pulled ten blocks away. Wilson Baker had cut the rope earlier that day. Was something brewing? Was it my responsibility to go or to stay?

I decided to go to Governor Collins's meeting, but for the briefest time possible. I wondered what he had to say from the president to the perhaps several hundred who might go.

As cars began arriving to take the clergy to the meeting, I discovered that I was having difficulty getting a ride. Each car seemed to have its passengers standing by, and off it would go. It appeared I would not get to the meeting after all. The more difficult it became, the more determined I was that I would go and hear Governor Collins.

I finally ungraciously squeezed myself into a car. Our car was followed to the rectory by a carload of Sheriff Clark's deputies, and there was not much conversation within our car as we watched the rear-view mirror.

The rectory was a more modern building than Brown Chapel. We were welcomed by a very clean-shaven and white-faced priest. It flashed through my mind that he and I made a strong contrast; I had the stubble of a new beard and my clothes had lost all their shape from the rain the night before. But we were on friendly turf—the church had over the months done its part in fostering voter registration, at the expense of great tension and some loss of members within its congregation.

To my surprise, I found the gathering to consist of only a handful of Protestant clergy and perhaps fifty Roman Catholic priests and nuns. Everyone's freshly scrubbed appearance, contrasted to my own and that of several black clergy, reminded me that some could have come from neighboring parishes and perhaps had not yet visited Sylvan Street.

I sat down in the main vestibule and immediately fell soundly asleep. Then I awoke to find that everyone had moved into a large meeting room. I stumbled in and was grateful to a black minister for pointing me to the only empty seat.

A piece of paper was circulating. I put my name on it, thinking I was signing a record of who was present. As it was passed around, I realized that I had signed a petition, a petition that had been read to the group once while I slept in the vestibule, and was now being read for the second time.

The petition was addressed to President Johnson from "the clergy in Selma" asking for a federalization of the National Guard, federally appointed registrars, and a quick redress of grievances through the federal court.

It was a good petition, as far as I could judge it. I was just surprised that I was learning about it at the moment it was to be handed to Governor Collins. I had signed it before I even knew it was a thought in anybody's head. The several Protestants around me confirmed that they had just heard of it at this meeting. None of us were at all sure that Dr. King or his associates were aware of it, and the meeting reeked of the kind of fragmentation we had been warned against again and again.

Governor Collins entered, and the petition was read to him in its entirety. He thanked us for our concern and said that while he could not speak for the president, he would be happy to deliver the petition, and he was certain that it would be given every consideration.

He then said that while we were assembled there we might like to know something about the Community Relations Service he headed, and the kinds of services it could provide in a situation like Selma's.

With those words, an alarm bell went off in my head that was earsplitting and silent at the same time. Here we were, about to be lectured to for perhaps two hours on the importance of his office, while bedlam threatened to break loose in the housing complex. Were we being manipulated like puppets by Jim Clark and his cohorts?

I immediately stood up and begged the pardon of the governor. I said that I had not realized what the nature of the meeting was to have been. I said that I felt that there was a very difficult situation back in Carver Houses that might break out at any moment, that we were undermanned there, and that I felt that I would have to excuse myself and go back to Brown Chapel.

An audible gasp went through the assembled clergy at my rudeness in the face of the president's appointed representative. Governor Collins was visibly shaken. He apologized for coming to the meeting and taking our valuable time, and headed for the door. The clergy rallied to his support and insisted that they had come there for exactly the purpose of hearing from him. Some looked at me in complete disdain.

As the governor stayed, I had to say one more thing. I apologized again for interrupting him, noting that I would not have thought myself capable of being rude to him, and that I was speaking for myself only. But I would have to be excused. The assemblage was happy to see me go.

A handful of local ministers joined me as I left. Fortunately one of them had a car; I hadn't stopped to think how I would get back. We drove through the dark night back to the activity of Sylvan Street.

The scene there was exactly as my mind had pictured it. As the several of us came up to the line demarking police and demonstrators, I could spot only one local minister in the center of the line, trying to hold people back. His first words were, "Boy, am I glad to see you fellas! You just got here in time." We interspersed ourselves among the activists and, by simply talking and being there, helped to calm things down a bit.

Having succeeded apparently in that, I turned and looked at the police line again, and now saw something that was completely astonishing to me. Behind the several lines of police standing shoulder to shoulder, their police cars were in a different configuration. For days they had occupied curbs and driveways on both sides of the street, facing the demonstrators. But there had always been one car dead center, sandwiched between two cars parked by the curbs. It visually presented a physical block to the marchers. It was the car from which Wilson Baker or Mayor Smitherman or whoever was in charge operated.

Now, that car was gone. In spite of the other police cars in their familiar spots, it presented a view of the road wide open to the marchers once they got around the standing policemen.

When I commented to several of the clergy about the car being absent, I was told that Wilson Baker was out looking for the missing clergy. This I found hard to believe. It was not that difficult to keep track of ministers in Selma, nor would Wilson Baker himself have to go on such an errand. If he had gone suddenly, it would have been logical for another car to take the place of his.

In the days that followed, I often discussed that moment in the history of Selma's demonstration. We were all of the opinion that Wilson Baker did not deliberately vacate that spot and leave the road open, because deep down we knew how seriously he took his job of maintaining the public peace. Looking back, however, I continued to feel that he had been, in fact, pulled away from that spot by a higher authority, that the road had been deliberately left open with the visiting clergy pulled out of harm's way, and that there had been a "gigantic plot" to have the demonstration go off half-cocked, resulting in injuries and death to the people left behind or racing to the courthouse. Whoever suggested to Governor Collins that he hold a meeting with the clergy in the Roman Catholic rectory was, I believed then and do today, out for blood.

Later that night, when absent adults had returned and the lines of confrontation were again more quietly in place, a small group of us Unitarian Universalist clergy held our own caucus in one of the homes. I was so fired by the events of the day, while having gone so long without sleep, that I could hardly stop talking. I also sensed that everybody there was worried about me in particular. I kept on talking and seemed to have all the answers to all the problems, yet logically knew this wasn't possible and that even as I spoke I was becoming the "basket case" I was afraid of becoming.

So, when somebody suggested that I simply go to bed, that they would see that our group was represented on the confrontation line all night long, I found myself happily concurring. I found a bed in the home of my second hostess, fell on it, and slept from about 12:30 to 6:00 a.m.

Day Six

Saturday, March 13. When morning came, my hostess encouraged me to take a bath. It was most welcome. On request, she also produced a much-needed deodorant. Sometime during the previous day I had found time to move my light travel bag from my then unguarded first lodging to my second one, so I could now put on a clean shirt and pair of socks. I was almost a new person. Only my shoes, caked with mud, soggy with rain, and wearing thin from marching, reminded me visually of the ordeal that was behind and the perhaps bigger one still ahead.

My ministerial colleagues were glad to see me back in good shape. Several priests came over to apologize for the previous night. It seems that a number had been new arrivals in Selma, and they had not fully estimated the volatility of the confrontation until I walked out of the meeting. They reported that many others had left soon after I did. They had also learned that Dr. King did not know of the petition; it had been tabled for further consideration and, to my knowledge, was never sent to the president.

Saturday began, for some reason, with a caucus of all the clergy of the various faiths in Brown Chapel. Some way had to be found to break the impasse with the police. An almost unanimous agreement was reached that several hundred clergy should lead an attempt in the afternoon to march to the courthouse.

At 1:00 p.m. we lined up five abreast with only clergy in the front ranks. Others who wanted to march came to the rear. The procession, singing "Onward, Christian Soldiers," was several hundred ranks long and very impressive as it marched toward the police line. The "church universal" was on the march, and few doubted that it would be triumphant.

Wilson Baker and a hundred helmeted police brought the church to a halt. In a weary voice the commissioner intoned that it was not conducive to the safety of the clergy or for the people in Selma for him to permit a march to the courthouse. As he finished those words, he undoubtedly expected the clergy to turn back or sit down or remain confronting the police line.

Instead, the clergy line veered in a sharp right turn and headed down between two buildings toward the courthouse, on a path that had not previously been taken by a unified group of marchers.

The police ran in all directions. Baker huffed and puffed to catch up with his policemen, who confronted the marchers again at a new line. Thoroughly schooled by now in nonviolent strategy, the clergy knew enough to stand still within two or three feet of the police and not try to force their way. The police moved forward slowly, in an effort to induce the demonstrators to back up or to panic and flee. But the clergy stood firm.

Baker found himself chest to chest with a clergyman. His voice bellowed out, "You're pushing me, you're pushing me! And you call yourself a man of God!" His voice trailed off in less audible mumbles.

He proceeded to arrest Rev. C. T. Vivian, the only black clergyman in the front rank. As he made the arrest, the clergymen on either side of Vivian locked arms with him and those on the outside file locked with the other three. It was a show of solidarity that must have surprised Baker and his men. In effect, the front rank was saying that if Baker was to arrest the one black, he would have to take them all.

Immediately the commissioner saw the error of his ways and released Rev. Vivian. This incident was later described as the quickest arrest and release in the history of Alabama.

However, the situation was still tense. Already clergymen several ranks back were organizing a march in another direction.

Suddenly from a window overlooking the crowd a huge voice boomed out asking everyone to listen. A minister had gone into the building to get a picture of the proceedings below and had accidentally overheard a radio account of the discussions going on between President Johnson and Governor Wallace at that very moment. The minister announced to the upturned faces that Johnson had just declared that he felt that the demonstrations on behalf of voting rights and against brutality were understandable and justified.

A mighty cheer went up from the demonstrators below, who again surprised the law enforcers by breaking ranks and walking calmly back to Brown Chapel to consider the implications of this welcome news. Once more the tension was relieved, and the stalemate returned to Sylvan Street.

If the police thought their busy afternoon was over and that the clergy, having had their run, would now relax on a pleasant Saturday afternoon to prepare for the sabbath, they were wrong.

About an hour later, around 3:00 p.m., the ministers, priests, rabbis, and nuns came pouring from the chapel again, arms linked with those of the black townspeople who wanted this time to march with them.

Instead of five abreast, they were now ten abreast, stretching all across Sylvan Street. A hundred or so police confronted them at the familiar line, and the march stopped. Almost immediately a group near the back of the procession broke off and moved in perfect order down between the two buildings the way the entire procession had gone an hour earlier. Naturally the police had to cover this area, so a line of police went running in that direction. The line held, and as always, the singing continued.

Then another group of clergy and protesters marched off in yet another direction and police were running in that direction to try to hold the line.

I was still at the point where the clothesline had once run, demarking the Selma Wall, looking at the main body of police eyeball to eyeball, and watching their growing consternation as they tried to hold the demonstration in check. By then it was apparent to them that our strategy was to apply pressure all the way around the project if possible, and to stretch the police lines as thin as they could possibly be stretched.

Signal after signal came to the police. Ten would run in one direction, a dozen would run in another. The ranks of the white, green, and blue helmets were all being thinned. Word came to us that if we could possibly get through the lines, we were to go in small groups and reassemble at the courthouse for our demonstration, a vigil, and the presentation of grievances.

In time, the police contained most of the demonstrators short of the courthouse. Some got through, however, and ran into an angry mob. Ken Marshall was with two youngsters not far from the courthouse when he was confronted by one green-helmeted posseman.

The minister and children stopped in their tracks, according to now well-practiced strategy, rather than try to run around him. The deputy glared at them. Ken said, with a certain presence of mind, "Well, we really have got you fellas working today, don't we?" The posseman, having trouble catching his breath, said, "Yes, you certainly do." All four stood firm. Then Ken and the children turned and walked back to the chapel. There had been a spark of communication between the two sides.

While most of the demonstrators were held within the perimeter of the black neighborhood, the police lines had been stretched to their maximum. I was still on the original line where I had started, holding hands with a black girl not more than 12 years old. She was obviously frightened, as indeed I was, but she was determined to be with us. Her zeal came out in freedom songs. Looking up at the police glaring down at her from three feet away, she sang one song after another for several hours, in the purest voice any of us had ever heard. It was too beautiful a sound for anyone else to want to add to, and for those several hours we saw not the slightest trace of emotion on the face of a single policeman. They simply looked at her, unbelieving that one small person could have that much energy.

Eventually the perimeter began to shrink as people returned to Sylvan Street. Some groups had faced angry crowds as well as the police. The few who made it to the courthouse had retreated in the face of hostility. Everyone gave credit to the press and the people holding TV cameras, who had moved as quickly as the demonstrators or the police, and whose presence in tense situations was often given credit for averting violence.

The news that President Johnson's sympathies were with us had boosted our morale considerably. But as I stood in the line that afternoon, with police running in all directions, it was easy to believe that mayhem could begin.

I also expected that this would be the moment when the federal government would have to intervene. I kept looking up in the air, thinking that we might see airplanes, even parachutists, as our government came to our rescue. But they didn't come.

The police re-established themselves at either end of Sylvan Street, and I found an opportunity to simply go into Brown Chapel, sit down, and collect my thoughts. I was sure that vast wheels must be in motion at this point. Governor Wallace must be being squeezed by the president on the one hand and by the Al Lingos and Jim Clarks on the other. SCLC and SNCC both must be changing their strategies for tomorrow and the next day.

As I sat, I could not think of a single meaningful thing I could do to help in the struggle. It was as if the whole issue had suddenly been taken out of the hands of the players. I guessed that the others must be feeling the same way. I could imagine Wilson Baker on the other side of the line saying, "Well, I've certainly done everything I can do—something has to give."

Was the die of history being cast at that moment, with no one knowing the outcome? Would the police, especially the state police, receive orders to break up the whole thing? Would tear gas come through a chapel window, as it had once while I was sitting in New York? Even now was an angry mob of whites massing in town to do their "demonstration" on the black community? Were troops on their way? Would I be alive at this time tomorrow?

All I could think to do was to think, and hope, and offer feeble prayers, and continue to write as much into my notes as I could. What were the "keys" to my situation? What had I learned?

Coincidence! The role of coincidence! The fact that I sat there in the Selma chapel rather than Don Harrington or Mel Van de Workeen by the coincidence that they had just been South and I had not. The coincidence that Jim Reeb had gone

44

to the restaurant and I had not. He was dead; I was still alive. The coincidence that I was only born because my mother, a nurse, had been assigned to my father as her first patient. The coincidence that I could have been born into the body of George Wallace, or the little girl who sang with me against the police that afternoon, or of a child who died in the first week of infancy on the other side of the world. Sweet mystery of life, as the song went. And of death.

Also, what these six days had shown me about people's capacities! I had found myself in a setting unlike anything I could possibly have imagined, in which thousands of people interplayed with each other in almost total absence of structure. Or was it structure that, paradoxically, changed from moment to moment?

The black community and the white clergy and supporters from the white communities had been thrown together and functioned with unbelievable efficiency, without benefit of committees, subcommittees, mimeo machines, telephones, anything that my ecclesiastical experience had told me was essential for getting things done.

If Dr. King, say, were taken out of the picture, briefly or forever, there was somebody equally eloquent to stand in his place. If a person performing a vital function anywhere had to leave, somebody was ready to step in. Ministers found themselves making sandwiches. Children found themselves marching. Would-be leaders found themselves being led. People like myself, who had come thinking that at best they would be good observers, while at the same time being counted, found themselves quickly enough being asked for leadership by those with a few hours' less experience. If the question were asked, Who is performing the most important job? or Who is in charge here? it would have been impossible to say.

While I sat musing in the church, the sexton came in and asked all the young people there to clean the church, which was very dirty indeed. The children sprang into action. Within ten minutes every scrap of paper was picked up, cushions were in place, clothing was folded, even brooms were hard at work. The place looked transformed. Perhaps the sexton was the most valuable person at that moment, because he saw what had to be done. An irate crowd breaking into the chapel then might be somewhat disarmed by seeing a lovely house of worship and children hard at work.

It was amusing too to think about the people who had arrived in Selma believing they were leaders, and who found that they could not lead. They usually took the next plane home. One man with army experience came for the purpose of "helping us organize." For him it was like trying to get a river back into its sources.

Perhaps we were experiencing pure democracy for the first time. One followed whom one respected, and ignored whom one didn't, whether the person was at a microphone or asking a favor on the street. Basically, the leaders were those who had the most experience. They knew what the alternatives might be, and the consequences, and we listened to them.

Occasionally I had found myself in a critical position in which my experience was clear and others begged for direction. So I gave it. If in doubt, and if possible, we were expected to check with someone with more experience, and I had done plenty of that. The length of the mass meetings in Brown Chapel derived from the clash of experience with experience, and everyone in his or her seat was learning quickly.

I marveled again at the lack of committees. There were no lists of people expected to do this, that, or the other thing. Many of the people could not read or write, but that fact seemed irrelevant; some of the most capable people had little or no formal education.

At times I became panicky at not seeing any well-known figures around in a difficult situation. But I came to realize that the leadership was never far away and in fact kept close touch.

Some of the SNCC leaders, I heard, were never seen, traveling back and forth between Mississippi, Alabama, and Georgia, organizing for the vote and trying to remain anonymous. Therefore, they would not be found standing eye to eye with the police on the front line, where pictures were continually taken for the police files and for the media nationally. They were more likely in someone's modest home discussing strategy.

46

At one point while ministers marched seven abreast down the road, I had recognized several SNCC workers on the sidewalk watching the march. I was for the moment furious that they were not in the front ranks with us. Then I remembered that this was, by agreement, a clergy march. Why shouldn't the church from time to time take its lumps and spare the heads of others?

As I thought about these things and still lacked any idea of what I could do constructively at that moment, the idea hit me that I could at least talk to the person sitting nearest me and get to know one Selma resident a little better. Perhaps her history belonged in my records.

So I asked her if she would mind being "sort of" interviewed. Many of both clergy and nonclergy had noted that I seemed always to be taking notes, even in tough situations. She cheerfully agreed to an interview.

I learned that she was thirteen years old, went to Henry Hudson High School in Selma, and that she wanted to either join the WACS or be a nurse when she grew up. Fried chicken was her favorite food. I noted that it must be everybody's favorite food around there because we had been served fried chicken once a day, at lunch or at supper, each of the days so far. Fortunately, it was also about my favorite food too. (The alternate lunch or dinner for us each day had as its main course "buffalo," not the kind that "play on the range" in the Midwest, but a type of fish that ran in great numbers in the Alabama River. It also was delicious.)

The more I talked with the youngster, the more I learned what a complete human being she was already at age thirteen. I asked her if she had gone across the bridge on the previous Sunday when the beatings took place. She had. I asked her how far she had been from the front rank on the march. She and her girlfriend had been the tenth rank of the group as it marched in pairs.

How did it feel? She had known beforehand that it was dangerous. The marchers had even been instructed about tear gas, and she confessed she had been mildly curious to know what tear gas was like. She had gone on the demonstration almost as a lark. But then all of a sudden the bridge loomed ahead of her and looked much bigger than she had ever remembered it. That, of course, corresponded exactly to my experience of the bridge.

Similarly, seeing the police waiting would be something she would never forget. She had not been beaten. But she had heard the cries and groans of the injured and had heard the wild shouting. She had also gotten the tear gas in her eyes and stumbled with her girlfriend back across the bridge.

Here she sat, ready to go again when the next march formed up. Though we were of the opposite sex, different races, far apart in age, with no real knowledge of the other's culture (she never out of Selma, me from sophisticated New York), we were expressing the identical feelings and ideas about human beings in general. Why, we asked, when people are so much alike, can't they get along better? At least in the Carver Houses we were finding that all people can make it together.

I talked to more people resting in Brown Chapel that evening. A subject that haunted me was how the idealism that we all expressed in pushing for equality and voting rights intersected with our concern for our individual safety, as well as the safety of the group. I found that, to a person, black and white, people had been drawn to Selma thinking of themselves as observers. Having observed, they were absolutely obliged to participate. Practically all admitted considerable concern about their individual welfare. Only two claimed never to have worried about their safety, and I think I was able to show those two that from time to time they had acted out of self-interest.

Honesty required me to say that in every situation that I had been in up to that point, I had been calculating alternatives, including the kinds of actions that would preserve my own safety. I speculated that the same must be true for Wilson Baker, each policeman, the deputy with the five-inch club, all the citizens of Selma. We were all doing what we had to do, and fear was a component for all.

While all the demonstrators professed their devotion to Dr. King's philosophy of nonviolence, most were a bit unsure how they should react if attacked. The idea was to maintain one's dignity as long as possible—when about to be struck, to fall down and assume a fetal position, protecting one's skull with arms and hands, and hope for the best. Bodies could protect bodies by huddling together. Women and children might thus be protected by men.

Most of us had gotten this message early in our meetings. Few would have been so foolish as to try to push past an angry policeman or citizen or to grapple with them. Beyond this basic strategy for meeting violence, we knew that each of us would be on our own, hopeful that in the end love could conquer hate.

The evening wore on. The chapel was not stormed. The federal troops did not arrive for our rescue. We took turns getting another meal in another church.

By 9:30 p.m. I was exhausted again and went to bed. But by 2:30 a.m. I was wide awake and concerned that our position against the police line might be deteriorating, so it was back to Sylvan Street.

There was always the problem of keeping enough people on the line to show our seriousness. Sometimes there were many hundred standing there in the middle of the night. This night, by about 4:00 a.m., we were down to fifty bodies, opposed by almost as many troopers, deputies, and police.

It was already Sunday. No doubt, everyone would be back on the line by the time the white townspeople of Selma entered their all-white congregations for worship.

Day Seven

Sunday, March 14. By that morning a heavy fog had rolled in, making it difficult to see any distance. As a new factor in everyone's calculations, it was something to worry about. Would whites bent on violence use this opportunity to slip into the black community to bomb or torch a target?

The sun came up, the fog burned off.

I found a chance to call home for the first time and spoke with my wife and each of my girls. They were in better spirits than I had expected to find them. But I had no answer to the question, "Daddy, when will you be home?"

49

Breakfast was with my hostess and her son. Occasionally we were able to have a meal together, and in the evening it could include her husband, a fisherman who went out at 4:00 a.m. to fish in the Alabama River. We were getting to know one another quite well.

The father took great pride in his job, and each day brought back about forty pounds of fish to be sold in the black community. It was, relatively speaking, a good living. Since I am generally partial to fish, I did not mind having fried "buffalo" for breakfast and again perhaps later in the day. It was very bony, but delicious.

When I moved in with this family I was interested in their seven-year-old. Initially I took an approach with him that had worked well with many other children, including my own. I tried to give him a job that would both help me and involve him more fully in what was going on.

I gave him seven dimes and asked him if he would try to make a newspaper collection for me, picking them up from the several places in town during the day and stacking them under the family TV. I could thus glean articles to take back to New York at the end of my stay.

He gladly accepted the challenge and left to get a newspaper. When he was gone, his mother told me that he had been arrested three times already by age seven. It seems that whenever people were getting arrested, he liked to go along to see what happened. One night he was forced by the police to stand for five hours bending over with both hands against a wall, as his punishment.

It was hard for me to believe that this youngster, so appealing in his personality, could already have a jail record. Or for that matter, that more than a third of Selma's adult black population had been in jail for their voting rights efforts. As I talked with my hostess, she opened up more and more about her experiences.

She said that she was among the fewer than four hundred blacks who so far had managed to get registered at the Dallas County Courthouse. One of the questions that had been put to her, in the "intelligence" section of her test was, "How many bubbles are there in a bar of soap?" It was small wonder that blacks saw the entire process as capricious, designed to put as few blacks on the rolls as possible.

She told me that in the beginning of the demonstrations, long before the beatings on the bridge that had brought us to Selma, five hundred blacks had been arrested at one time and herded into a barn. There they were forced to stand all night because of their great number. The only light and air came through cracks above the door. Toilet facilities were improvised near the back of the barn.

Among the five hundred held those hours was an eighty-year-old man and his seventy-five-year-old wife. They stood all night. On top of that, the man had a case of the flu, and of course everyone worried about him. But several weeks later he was back in church and proudly announced that he thought the experience had cured him of the flu.

These kinds of stories were told over and over again by the people from their firsthand experiences. The most moving story was told by Rev. C. T. Vivian about the killing of Jimmy Lee Jackson in nearby Marion in February. Vivian had gone to Marion to speak. Later, a march was attempted, which was broken up by the police swinging their clubs. Jimmy Lee, his mother, and his grandfather were forced into a cafe for safety, but the police followed them in, injuring both his mother and his grandfather. When Jackson tried to intervene, he was shot at point-blank range. He clung to life for two weeks in a Selma hospital before dying. The march the previous Sunday was an attempt to protest the death of Jimmy Lee Jackson. In the black community Jackson was every bit the martyr that James Reeb was, and whites who forgot that fact lost communication with the blacks.

As I had stood on the line the previous night, I had noticed a new figure sitting in one of the lead police cars, in a dark uniform with lots of gold braid. He had looked even amiable, and some of us thought the police might be mellowing a bit under our bombardment of freedom songs. When I mentioned him to my hostess at breakfast, she said, "Yes, we know who he is; he's the man who shot a Negro, tied him to the bumper of his car, and dragged him around town for everyone to see."

Interwoven into these remembrances were stories told in the chapel or while we stood on the line that everyone recognized as jokes and parodies of the blacks' situation. James Bevel told about the white driver from the North who was passing through Alabama one night at about eighty miles an hour. Too late he saw two black men whom he could not avoid hitting. In the crash, one came through the windshield into the front seat, the other was knocked high into a tree and dangled there. When the police arrived, the driver was wringing his hands and moaning, "My God, what have I done? I was speeding and I've hit two people!" The policeman, noting that both victims were black, said, "It's all right. I'll book one of them for breaking and entering and the other for leaving the scene of an accident."

When I went back to the Selma Wall that morning, I found that the line was being maintained by the police with the aid of wooden barricades. The fact that it was Sunday made me think that this day might be different from the previous ones. I mentioned my hope to a friend, who said, "Don't forget what happened last Sunday," a reminder that brutality doesn't necessarily take a holiday.

The ministers met early in Brown Chapel and decided they would march again. This time they hoped to visit some of the all-white churches of the city. Again, they were stopped in their tracks by Wilson Baker, but with a new message.

He announced that if the clergy of the various faiths wanted to go in small groups to their churches with their friends, they could do so. This called for a strategy meeting back in the chapel, and the decision was made to accept the offer. Each group, however, would have at least one black in it.

There was no Unitarian Universalist church in Selma, so I decided to go with the Episcopalians to their church in town. Fifteen of us set out together walking. In our group were several black and white Episcopal clergy, a young black Episcopal girl, and other Episcopalians, black and white.

We were careful to cross streets with the light, not step off curbs when the light was against us, and not walk on lawns or commit other possible infractions. Several police cars kept abreast of us all the way to the church, possibly to protect us from groups that stared at us from the other side of the street.

On arriving at the church, our young Episcopal minister, Morris Samuels, led us up the walk to the main entry. There four church elders stood shoulder to shoulder blocking our way, in the identical posture of the police at the Selma Wall.

When we asked if we could enter their church to worship that morning, we were told that they would admit any Episcopalian clergy, but no one else. We stated that there were nonclergy Episcopalians among us. But the offer did not change. One of the elders made a reference to our "publicity stunt." We assured them that while several newsmen had chosen to accompany us, we had come to join the congregation in worship.

Failing entrance for our group of fifteen, our Episcopal priest led us in a moving worship service on the front lawn of the church. It lasted about twenty minutes. Three members of the local congregation, arriving for church and finding that we had been barred at the door, refused to go into their own church to worship and joined us on the lawn. Another invited us to come back after the service or to send a delegation to talk with their vestry. One woman congregant said, "If I was in charge of the vestry, you'd get in."

We walked from the Episcopal church back to Sylvan Street without incident, again obeying traffic lights carefully. Even then several cars drove needlessly close to us, as a form of harassment. We had toyed with going to a second church, but since their service would now already be in progress and our arrival would be a serious disruption, we elected to continue our worship in Brown Chapel.

The afternoon brought out a strong sun and warm temperatures. The line stood many ranks deep facing the police, who were now on the other side of the wooden barricades.

Buses were arriving with new people to support the tired veterans of the Selma Wall. A number of the new people were

Unitarian Universalists, coming to attend a memorial service Monday for their fallen clergyman, Jim Reeb.

Many of the new arrivals were college students, some on a lark, rating several days in Selma as an interesting spring break. One young man whose T-shirt boldly proclaimed HARVARD on it, carried a sign with big letters reading I AM A COMMUNIST AGITATOR. He was getting many laughs from other newly arrived college types, and he began to walk with his sign toward the police lines.

I made an instant decision that, with newsmen at the line looking harder now for news stories, and with Governor Wallace and the Jim Clarks of the world sure that our movement was riddled with "commie sympathizers," this practical joker should not show his sign to either the press or the police. I interposed myself directly in front of him, in the manner of an enforcement officer, and said, "I cannot permit you to send this message unless you have cleared it with the Student Nonviolent Coordinating Committee." He admitted that he had cleared his sign with no one, and that was the last we saw of that sign.

Meanwhile, dignitaries were arriving from all over. They, of course, walked up to the front of the line. Some were encouraged to speak, and not all of them got a good response from the crowd. Particularly offensive were white ministers who talked of the death of Jim Reeb without linking it in any meaningful way to the deaths of countless blacks in Alabama.

Union President Walter Reuther appeared as if by magic opposite the police and spoke with great warmth and conviction about the economic side of the blacks' struggle. He was immediately followed by a young black male, not more than twenty, who spoke with such eloquence that Reuther's mouth hung open. When the young man finished, Reuther grasped his hand in gratitude and admiration.

The police, simply by their presence, were forced to hear, hour after hour, a different point of view than the one they had grown up with. From Dr. King, Hosea Williams, Jim Bevel, Ralph Abernathy, to the heads of nationwide church denominations, to the Rosa Parkses of the South, all challenged the established authorities in the name of a more just society. I wondered if any of the police found any thought from the demonstrators disturbing to their own view of the world. If they did, they did not show it.

Hosea Williams spoke of the high rate of illegitimacy among blacks being traceable to slavery days, when black families could not afford to be as tightly bound to one another as the whites because their children could be taken away and sold to other slave owners, as could the adults. "The whites trained our families not to love too much," he said. "The basic problem today is that Negroes are not fully people in the thinking of whites."

As speeches, prayers, and songs continued, preparations were underway for the memorial service the next day. The entire Board of Trustees of the Unitarian Universalist Association, thirty-strong, was arriving in Selma that afternoon, along with staff members from Boston and members of local congregations around the country. I wondered what kind of a view they would have of Selma and the demonstration if they came and went within twenty-four hours.

The UUA board was to be housed in the Catholic rectory ten blocks away, where two nights before I had had my emotional confrontation with Governor Collins. Now I was welcoming my fellow UUs and helping organize a three-car convoy to get the vanguard of the board to the rectory.

At last three cars set off for the ten-block trip. I was in the third car. The driver of the first car surprisingly took us down a main street in the white neighborhood. The next thing I knew, a railroad crossing gate was coming down, separating us from the other two cars. We had to stop, while they went on. As we sat watching a slow freight pass for what seemed an interminable time, our driver noted that a carload of sheriff's deputies had pulled up behind us. I suggested we not look around. Meanwhile we glanced out of the side windows to see if angry whites were gathering on the street. It was easy for me to believe that some diabolical hand had sorted us out to be the next victims.

The crossing gate went up. The car behind us sped past. We had apparently not been recognized as clergy-visitors. Also I realized that it was a state trooper's car, full of blue helmets, not a sheriff's car with green helmets, passing that information on to our driver and our new arrivals, who had not yet mastered the significance of the different colored helmets.

Another mass meeting was planned for 7:30 p.m. in Brown Chapel. When 7:30 arrived, the chapel was again packed to its limits, including its windows and vestibules, with several hundred unable to get in. UUA President Dana Greeley sat with Dr. King and a number of speakers on the platform.

As the meeting was about to begin, I was able to get close to Dr. Greeley. I whispered in his ear, "If you are going to speak, make sure that you never mention James Reeb without mentioning Jimmy Lee Jackson in the same breath—they are both martyrs in everyone's eyes, and to only talk of Reeb is to display our own racism." He got the point immediately and seemed very grateful to me. When he later addressed the huge congregation, Jimmy Lee Jackson and James Reeb were treated as brothers, which they were.

As part of the worship service that preceded the meeting, an offering was taken. Every inch of space seemed occupied by a human being. The business of taking up an offering lasted a full hour, with other things happening while the plates were passed. But first the "special" offerings were taken up, offerings by individuals representing groups. Lines of givers formed on either side of the church. Each person who came forward identified himself or herself with the group represented. Gifts ranged from $1 to $500.

Following the special offerings, the plates were passed for the smaller offerings. Much later the presiding minister asked if anyone wished to make an offering who had not done so. Several called from the balcony that the plates had not made it to them. The prospect of getting plates to the balcony in the crush of people looked dim, and the next thing we knew, bills and coins were raining down from the balcony onto the surprised people below. The money was gathered off the floor and passed forward.

The front row of the church had been occupied almost solely by Unitarian Universalist ministers and trustees, who to a person watched the bills floating down and the coins bouncing on the floor in complete disbelief. A new chapter was being written in the history of church fund-raising.

The speakers welcomed the great number of new arrivals. Newcomers were told that in addition to attending the memorial service the next day, they would also have the opportunity to go to jail if they wished to participate in the demonstrations. "You should not feel guilty if you have other commitments that keep you out of jail, nor should anyone feel superior just because he or she has nothing better to do than go to jail," a speaker advised.

The visitors were also asked not to take unfair advantage of the hospitality offered by the people of the community. Whenever possible, visitors should sleep on the floor and let the hosts and hostesses sleep in their own beds. If things were not as organized or as clean as they might wish, "Remember that we are involved, not in a war on uncleanliness, but in a war on segregation."

James Bevel added that tomorrow there was a possibility for the first time of more whites being arrested than blacks; this would be a source of considerable embarrassment to the state of Alabama.

One of the newly arrived Unitarian Universalists was eighty-four-year-old Judge Lawrence Brooks of Massachusetts, the parliamentarian of the denomination, a man who carried himself with surpassing dignity. It had been decided that he would not stay for the entire meeting, which was entering its third hour. I offered to escort him out of the crowded church to his lodgings.

As we reached the front door of Brown Chapel, he asked if he could see the place where the police and demonstrators had confronted each other for almost a week, and I was pleased to be able to walk him past the ranks of demonstrators to the head of the line.

It had been raining again, and we slowly walked around and through puddles up to the wooden barricade. With floodlights playing down and police headlights shining in our eyes, I tried to see the scene through the eyes of the distinguished American jurist.

It was an eerie and frightening sight, heightened by the light rain. He placed both hands firmly on the wooden barrier, looked straight at the police, and said, "I can't believe that this could ever happen in America."

We turned to leave, and I found myself telling him the story of the eighty-year-old man and his seventy-five-year-old wife who had had to stand in the barn all night, the man later claiming that the experience had cured him of the flu. Somehow it was becoming necessary for me to relate to each incoming white person the sufferings of the blacks in Selma, as well as their remarkable good humor and determination to "be free," that is, to have the right to vote.

Following that long meeting it was felt necessary to have another "orientation" meeting for all the newcomers. These sessions were simply workshops on how to defend oneself if attacked. Rolled up newspapers were used as billy clubs. We took turns falling to the floor and shielding our skulls.

Some of the newcomers walked out of the orientation while valuable information on survival was being given. Like almost every newcomer, they were underestimating the dangers of their situation. Following the orientation session, I took another turn on the line, in the rain. Then I headed to bed, letting others have their experience of standing and singing through the night.

Day Eight

Monday, March 15. When I awoke at 6:00 a.m., I felt as though I had had the sleep of a Rip Van Winkle. I lay in bed first feeling completely contented, then felt that same wave of fear that came across me each time I awoke in Selma, the fear that disaster was impending, that this might be the last day for some or many of us.

When this wave had passed, I lay in bed a while longer, thinking about how everyone's safety appeared related to everyone else's. Once we had been drawn into the Selma whirlwind, there was no exit for the individual acting alone without abdicating safety and probably responsibility.

But sticking together did not guarantee safety either. One did not know where danger lurked. A "sanctuary" like the rectory ten blocks away could be the very target of violence. A parade of marchers heading out into the white community could be safer than those left behind in the black housing. Someone walking next to you could have been planted there by the police.

However, this feeling of continually living with danger was not unlike the continuous experience of blacks living in a place like Selma.

There was a certain irony for me in the instruction we had received to only go into the white neighborhoods during the day if we had to and not at night except when absolutely necessary. I could not help comparing it with instruction often given to whites in the North not to go into Harlem, for example, after dark. In Selma it was in the white community where violence lurked.

The previous day had given us a pointed illustration. A little black girl had been taken to a clinic in the white neighborhood. While she was there, her driver was arrested for not carrying his car registration, and he was taken away. Word immediately went out to the black community not to let the little girl walk out of the clinic by herself, since night was coming. Rather, a black priest courageously went to the clinic and brought the little girl back.

As I headed toward Brown Chapel early that morning, high school boys were already on an outdoor basketball court playing the game as hard as they knew how. I paused to watch them and consider their role in the struggle we were in. Whenever there had been a march, a few would leave the court to join the marchers. But the majority would go on playing basketball while citizens and clergy lined up alongside them. Was this irresponsible? Were they playing it "safe" in their own way? Perhaps. But I was also glad that not all the able-bodied men left the community when there was a demonstration. Just a glimpse of some of the six-footers playing basketball might be enough to discourage mischief from the outside.

When I got to the line that morning, I was amazed to find that there was no line. The wooden barricade had been removed at 6:15, I was told, and the police had vanished as if swallowed up by the earth. It was gratifying to be able to look down the open road, but also a bit disconcerting to know that any number of angry people might come from the other direction.

The ministers were assembling in Brown Chapel by 7:30. Their decision was to march on the courthouse and test whether the city was actually granting us the right to have a peaceful demonstration there. They were told that if they were arrested, they would probably miss the memorial service that afternoon, but that the service would undoubtedly have more meaning if a number of the clergy were in jail.

By 9:30 we had lined up on the street and set off for the courthouse. At the end of the block, in their familiar spot, the police reappeared as mysteriously as they had disappeared. Once more we were told that it was "not conducive to the safety of the townspeople" or ourselves to attempt this march. The ministers thereupon sang hymns, had a prayer, and returned to the church.

The memorial service had been scheduled for 2:00 p.m. At 2:00 p.m. the church was full. But there was no sign of Dr. King or several other leaders who were expected. The temperature in the church continued to mount. I could see the distress on the faces of my Unitarian Universalist friends as they kept looking at their watches, perhaps with planes to meet later in the day. For the rest of us, "seasoned veterans" of a week in Selma, we could have predicted that the service would start about 3:00, in keeping with the pattern of announcing meetings to start ahead of the actual starting time so that everybody would have a chance to get there.

At 3:00 p.m. Dr. King arrived, amid cheers outdoors and then in the church. From the moment the service began, I found myself greatly agitated and sometimes furiously angry at the behavior of my white colleagues.

From the balcony I saw a sea of dignitaries clearly unrelated to the events in Selma. Many faiths had come to pay tribute in this memorial to Jim Reeb. There was a certain uplift that came from the broad spectrum participating in this ecumenical service.

Beyond that, until Dr. King himself spoke, it is hard to imagine a more jumbled collection of prepared prayers and speeches rattled off in a patronizing way. It was ecclesiasticism at its worst. James Reeb's death was described as the most monstrous example of brutality, when in fact it was one more instance in a long series. Men who had not taken the time to meet any young people praised them for their courage. The men and women who had come "thousands of miles" for the memorial were extolled. I thought that it was not too difficult to come and go in twenty-four hours and have the vicarious experience of heroism through the experience of singing a few freedom songs.

At one point I heard freedom songs coming from outdoors, probably at the symbolic "line" now dissolved, and wondered if anyone inside the church was annoyed that songs were coming from outside the church. Pictures were being taken right and left. I mellowed a bit when I saw a photograph being taken by Orloff Miller, one of the three ministers attacked with Reeb outside Walker's Cafe.

When King began to speak, however, it suddenly seemed right that we should all be there. Everyone moved a bit in his or her seat when King asked rhetorically, "Who killed Jim Reeb?" He answered, "A few ignorant men." He then asked, "What killed Jim Reeb?" and answered, "An irrelevant church, an indifferent clergy, an irresponsible political system, a corrupt law enforcement hierarchy, a timid federal government, and an uncommitted Negro population."

He exhorted us to "leave the ivory towers of learning and storm the bastions of segregation," and see to it that the work Jim Reeb had started be continued so that the White South might come to terms with its conscience. He concluded with the quotation from Hamlet: "Good night, sweet prince, and flights of angels sing thee to thy rest."

We rose to sing "We Shall Overcome" yet one more time, and close to a thousand voices united in a mighty chorus. The verse "Black and white together" took on a deeper meaning for us as we thought of Jimmy Lee Jackson and James Reeb united in the democracy of death. Then, as we hummed a final chorus of the song, the Hebrew prayer for the dead was intoned and then translated for us, with its phrase, "Peace for all with justice."

At the conclusion of the service a new figure appeared at the microphone to make the electrifying announcement that the federal court had upheld our right to march to the courthouse and hold a service there.

A mighty cheer went up, and we tumbled out of the chapel to form our lines once more. Close to three thousand marchers lined up on Sylvan Street. This time, as we drew up to the police presence, we were told that we would be permitted to march if we stayed on the sidewalks where possible and marched three abreast. This we were willing to do, and the procession was on its way.

The sight of thousands of marchers passing three abreast through the town after the demonstrations had been contained for seven days must have been a considerable surprise to the other residents of Selma. We were escorted all the way by police cars while angry people muttered on the other side of the street. We arrived without serious incident at the Dallas County Courthouse.

On the march I found myself holding the hands of two young boys, one Clarence Jones, age thirteen, the other Clarence Young, age nine. Amateur and professional photographers were taking pictures as fast as they could load their cameras. I could not help thinking that if a picture of me and the two young black boys got back to the Community Church in New York, all there would be pleased to see me looking after two children.

The idea that I was protecting the boys, however, would have been erroneous. We had long since learned that in the event of trouble, the children were much faster and much more alert than adults, and knew how to protect themselves much better than adults. In effect, these children were protecting me more than I was protecting them.

The crowd of demonstrators that gathered in front of the courthouse was so huge that most of us were unable to hear the statements being read on the steps. Some were able to listen to the statements on their transistor radios. I could not help but notice one young black man who preferred to listen to a baseball game rather than the impassioned statements. A few pipe-smoking sophisticates from the North also looked out of place. Sheriff Clark was understood to be in the building, but may not have bothered to look out his window.

Darkness was falling rapidly as the last of the three thousand demonstrators reentered the Carver Houses that night. The sense of victory was heavy in the air. A march on Montgomery no longer seemed like an unrealizable dream. Relaxing was possible.

In addition, the president of the United States was to speak on television that night. By 9:00 p.m. every television set in the Carver Houses was banked with as many persons as could squeeze into the room. Johnson began: "At times history and fate meet in a single time in a single place to shape a turning point in man's unending search for freedom. So it was at Lexington and Concord. So it was a century ago at Appomattox. So it was last week in Selma, Alabama."

Forty-five minutes later he concluded his ringing address to Congress, in which he had urged Congress to help him pass a new voting rights bill. Everyone in the room where we had stood throughout was crying—men and women, old and young, black and white.

That night there was no line to confront at the end of Sylvan Street. The police were conspicuous by their scarcity. Two questions remained: Would Congress pass the new Voting Rights Bill, and more immediately now on many of our minds, would we get the permission we sought from the federal government to march the fifty miles to Montgomery to present our grievances to George Wallace?

Day Nine

Tuesday, March 16. The next day an air of great optimism continued through the whole community. There was a rumor that six thousand federal marshals were on the way to Selma. We heard other rumors of parked cars containing unidentified men, who must be there to protect us. (In actual fact, the president at no time had more than a hundred marshals in Selma. But we eagerly believed that there were sixty times that number.)

There was still the possibility of a bombing, or a parade of angry white citizens in a counter-demonstration through Sylvan Street. But we found ourselves relaxing to a degree.

For something to do, I visited a small building near the chapel that served as headquarters for the housing development itself. The black manager on duty was most cordial toward me and surprised me by inviting me to look over the rental charts or any other information that I might find interesting.

I spent a few minutes in his office and had begun to talk to two of his black employees when I was confronted by a white man, the overseer of the whole operation. His face, inches from mine, was twisted in seething anger. Somehow he managed to get out the words that he did not want me to interfere with the employees, who should be working. I assured him very politely that I had no intention of disturbing the management or the employees, and made my exit. Later, when I saw the manager I had talked to first, I said that I hoped my presence had not gotten him into trouble. He assured me that it had not. I wondered.

That day attention shifted nationally from Selma to Montgomery, where several large demonstrations were in progress also, protesting police brutality and in favor of voting rights. A number of our ministers had gone to Montgomery to add their support. I remained in Selma, in a new role that had suddenly developed and to which I felt suited, serving as a telephone contact in Selma for all the Unitarian Universalists nationally who were coming and going from the town in great numbers, and whose movements, particularly on the road between Montgomery and Selma, needed careful tracking because of the danger involved.

In Montgomery our ministers Roy Mersky and Ed Seiverts were only a few yards away from a group that was attacked by the police for demonstrating without a permit. Ed Seiverts told me afterwards that he could not believe what he saw, that the city police of Montgomery had held protesters, almost all of whom were black, in a pocket until the county deputies rode in on their horses and began beating the demonstrators. Two or three horses would be used to maneuver a demonstrator into a pocket where he could be beaten by more than one horseman at the same time. If he or she fell, the person was in great danger of being trampled by the horses. Clubs and whips were both used liberally by the deputies. This act of brutality fortunately was captured by TV cameras, shown nationally, and later called a "mistake" by state officials.

In Selma word was going around that the buying of guns had risen dramatically that week. It was obvious that they were not being sold to blacks. A black couple testified that they had been shot at the previous night only two blocks from the Carver Houses.

Orientation sessions continued for new arrivals. At 5:00 p.m., after another meeting, the ministers were ready to march again to the courthouse, this time to protest the violence we were hearing about in Montgomery. The opinion was that our previous march to the courthouse had been under a federal edict, and that we had not really tested the city on our right to demonstrate peacefully on Selma's streets. It was also suggested that the marchers consist of newly arrived clergy, or those who would be going home soon.

The march began and got as far as the now familiar Selma Line at the end of the block before it was stopped by the police, this time without benefit of rope or wooden barriers. This group of protesters gave ground, abandoned the line, and retired to the chapel. For the first time, police cars drove back and forth on Sylvan Street, an ominous development, with the purpose of deterring further marches.

Inside the chapel the ministers discussed what their strategy should be and decided to try another march, even with the presence of police cars in front of the chapel.

This time the clergy got only as far as the sidewalk directly in front of the chapel before they were faced by Wilson Baker and the police and told not to try any more demonstrations. To emphasize his determination, Baker tried to cordon off an area around the front of the chapel with another clothesline. But as he got the rope stretched about halfway around the clergy, a small black boy neatly cut the rope where it was first tied. Enraged, Commissioner Baker came back around to find who had cut the line. Immediately, another boy stepped forward and permitted himself to be searched, while the culprit with the scissors slipped easily into the crowd. Wilson Baker gave up his attempt to tie us in, and the milling crowd on the chapel steps, faced with the police, gradually settled down to singing songs with a guitar accompaniment and making speeches into their microphone.

Tension gradually abated. Around 9:00 p.m. the police had left. They knew we would not attempt a march at night.

I found myself actually sitting on a lawn, in an easy chair, within earshot of some long-distance calls, looking at a full moon and beautiful clouds moving in a light breeze. The singing of freedom songs continued in the distance. Inside the apartment behind me, several bottles of bourbon were being knocked off by a crowd of adults. It seemed as though the evening was about as peaceful as it could get—complete, however, with fifty police-men in their cars around Sylvan Street.

Day Ten

Wednesday, March 17. The next day, St. Patrick's Day, was also the eighth birthday of my daughter Elizabeth. I telephoned home around 7:30 a.m. and spoke with the whole family, telling Elizabeth that my present to her would have to be my coming home "before much longer."

I felt, in fact, a great urge to pull up stakes then and there and head for the Montgomery Airport. I had developed a severe cold in the last few days, and now it was becoming a hacking cough. In addition, the big toe on my right foot was giving me a serious problem. I had injured it carelessly the morning that I later dis-covered I was heading to Selma. It had not completely healed, exposed as it was to the off-and-on rain and soggy, warped shoes. The toe did not appear to be infected, but it had become quite numb. I did not want to go outside the black community for medical attention.

I decided that, if possible, I would not march that day, that I would try to eat a great deal and sleep more than I had been sleeping. By conserving what strength I had left, I might eventually be able to make the march to Montgomery. That culminating march was more and more on everyone's mind, as the tide of federal involvement seemed to be swinging toward us.

We received word from Commissioner Baker that morning that we would be permitted to march to the courthouse at 2:00 p.m. In addition, we planned to send groups of clergy and residents of Dallas County to other counties to support people there in their attempts to register for voting. Some of our Unitarian Universalist ministers went to other counties that day.

I spent much of the morning making and answering long-distance telephone calls. Our congregations all over the country were seeking direction on how they could best serve. We were alerting them not to come to Selma immediately, where the large number of visitors was straining hospitality, but rather to meet us for the march itself or even the last leg of the march into Montgomery, if and when it occurred. Already more than a hundred Unitarian Universalists had passed through Selma, and I was busy keeping that record, as well as a record of those who were leaving for good, and those who were going and coming for demonstrations in other counties.

My record-keeping had become a sort of private chess game, with very serious overtones, however, since there was always the possibility that someone would disappear off the chart and perhaps not be found until months later, as had happened to the three young civil rights workers in Mississippi.

That morning I also spent some time with the children of the neighborhood. One girl, age twelve, told me that she was studying medieval history in school. On further inquiry I found that she had been out of Selma only twice that she could remember, and then to two neighboring towns. The contrast between her subject in school and her practical experience was incredible.

I became more and more interested in how the subject of geography related to the young blacks of Selma. I found no young person who could draw the simplest map of the city, much less of the state or the world. In fact, none of them could recall ever seeing a map of Selma. They knew only the streets in their own neighborhood.

That morning a special delivery package arrived for me from New York. I was surprised and delighted to find in it a pair of heavy woolen socks from the staff of the Community Church, along with some candy bars I could nibble on during a march to Montgomery. It was impossible to express how much this thoughtful gift from my church meant to me at that moment. If I had wavered in my desire to march the fifty miles to the capital, my goal was now firmly in place.

I caught a glimpse of one of the policemen reading the latest *Life* magazine. Knowing that it must have a story, and perhaps many good pictures, of the events in Selma, I determined to get a copy for our now so-called "Unitarian Universalist Headquarters," located in a private house. But it appeared that *Life* magazine could not be obtained within the black community. I found a willing young man and promised him $5 if he could somehow get us the current issue. I would collect the $5 from my clergy friends. An hour later he was back with our magazine, which we all read avidly, and he received his $5.

Soon the word got around among the children that our "headquarters" had money and was fair game, because after the magazine episode, children came by simply asking for handouts. I could honestly tell them that I might very well need any money I had while I was in Alabama.

As I walked in front of Brown Chapel, a huge transcontinental bus pulled up and unloaded ninety of the cleanest, best-looking people I have ever seen, blacks and whites. The bus had driven all the way from Connecticut, and the newcomers were greeted as if they were both long-lost relatives and the rescue force of a beleaguered outpost, at one and the same time.

By 2:00 p.m. quite a few hundred people had lined up on Sylvan Street to make the daily march to the courthouse. The sky was darkly overcast. Remembering my decision not to march that day for reasons of health, I had very mixed feelings as I watched them head down the road to make their demonstration. They were no sooner out of sight than the heavens opened up in another torrential rain, quite in keeping with the script that we had been following. Truthfully I could not help thinking that it was rather fitting for these newcomers to receive *their* baptism by immersion, something that came to each of us in turn. Later, as they straggled back into the project, I congratulated myself on having let somebody else do the marching that day.

That afternoon there were more orientation sessions at the Baptist Church. Many of us had been over this ground a number of times and were amused when one person stood up and asked, "What do you do when you are shot?" The answer from our workshop leader was, "Try to fall down. And if your skin is broken, see if you can bleed."

Another mass meeting took place at 7:30 p.m. Speaker after speaker stressed the events in Selma as being pivotal to the struggle for human dignity everywhere. There was much discussion of what religion is all about. One black preacher said he used to have trouble filling his church. The previous Sunday he had seen two black boys in his congregation helping a white girl into the church through a window because of the crowd. It was something he could not have imagined happening. He noted that "when Christianity is relevant, people will come through the church windows."

Another speaker took a poke at the traditional observance of Brotherhood Week, which he called a "tea and cookie-pushing formality." "God is moving here in history here in Selma," he said, "to make humans more human." Silently we agreed that it must be a crucial week in American history.

Following the mass meeting we held an informal caucus of on-site Unitarian Universalists. When my hostess offered me a cold beer, I thought about my cold and my hacking cough and the fact that I had no medicine to counteract them. I guessed that a little alcohol would probably do me good. That night I managed almost seven hours of sleep.

Day Eleven

Thursday, March 18. Thursday I awoke feeling much better. On the way to breakfast I found the now familiar boys playing basketball on the outdoor court. They welcomed me to join them. It was in all likelihood their first experience playing on the same court with a white person. We discovered together that basketball is basketball, in any color, black or white or mixed.

The morning meeting in Brown Chapel was electric with the news that U.S. District Judge Frank Johnson had issued an order permitting the march from Selma to Montgomery, and ordering that it be given protection both by the state and the federal governments. The march could begin on Sunday.

Everyone's emotion gave way, in applause, cheers, tears, hugs, and dancing. The song "Ain't Gonna Let Nobody Turn Me 'Round" rang through the chapel and out into Sylvan Street.

The judge, however, had imposed some qualifications on the march, which SCLC had accepted in the interest of making the march manageable even from SCLC's point of view. Not everybody would be able to march the entire distance of fifty miles. Much of the route would be through the very rural Lowndes County, where Route 80 changed from a four-lane highway to two lanes. Moving thousands of people along those two lanes for several days, while traffic needed to pass through, was a prescription not only for confusion and impasse, but also for violent confrontation.

Judge Johnson ruled that as many as wished could march until the road became two lanes. Then only three hundred people would be allowed to continue, until the road opened up into four lanes again west of Montgomery, where again, no limit would be imposed.

Everyone was jubilant. It was yet to be determined how the three hundred people would be selected to march the fifty miles. But there was no question in my mind but that three hundred was a big number, and I surely would be among that group.

By late afternoon our telephone operation had reached a new pitch of activity. We had Unitarian Universalist "command posts" in Selma, Montgomery, Birmingham, and at the Montgomery Airport. Now it was time for everybody with the inclination, not just clergy, to descend on Selma and show the world that people of goodwill, of all colors, could unite behind the ideals of brotherhood and racial equality. Should they start south today? Good sense said, Wait for the next advisory.

Around lunchtime I passed Brown Chapel and was shown a piece of literature defaming Martin Luther King Jr. It had been handed out of a police car across the street from the chapel. Not wanting to go away empty-handed, I went to the car and asked if they had any more of the pieces. They said they did not. When I returned to the other side of the street, the man who had shown me the original flier said, "He's lying—he's got a whole stack of them on his lap. He's resting his arm on them."

Apparently the police had thought they had come up with some startling expose capable of wrecking our movement and sending us reeling in confusion. They were surprised that everyone wanted a copy, as a souvenir.

Around 3:00 p.m. I called my church in New York again to thank them for my package and to reassure them that all was going well, that of course I wanted to, indeed would have to, remain in Selma and walk the fifty miles, but that others apparently could now join us at either end of the march if they chose.

The day concluded with another packed and enthusiastic meeting in Brown Chapel, and for me, two beers and six hours of sleep. It was time to think about next week's "March to Freedom."

Day Twelve

Friday, March 19. On my way to breakfast in the morning I found some children playing touch football. I watched awhile. They invited me into their game, and I played long enough to get winded and show my age.

Sitting on the ground later, relaxing, I was approached by a little girl not older than four. I had seen this child before, and I smiled at her. Without warning she reached back and hit me across the face as hard as a four-year-old could possibly hit.

71

While the blow didn't loosen any teeth, it stung and knocked my glasses askew.

I reacted automatically, grabbing her small arms in my big hands, looking her right in the eyes, and saying sternly, "Don't you ever do that again." She immediately became sullen and withdrawn, but did not run away or cry.

As we warily looked at each other, with our heads about on the same level, I had plenty of time to contemplate how the non-violent movement in Selma related to a four-year-old black child. Was I the first white person this child had close contact with? Was her action possibly not even related to a perceived "lack of color" on my part?

I resolved to pursue the matter a bit further by engaging her in games and letting her think I had forgotten her aggressive act. Before long I evoked a smile from her. But there was a residue of feeling on her part. If I simply touched her finger, she enjoyed pretending that I had hurt her. Perhaps realizing that she had hurt me, she wanted to even things by letting me know she could be hurt also. Perhaps it was an adult-child thing, not a black-white thing. I still felt that, given the tensions in Selma, which were undoubtedly affecting every household, race played a part in her act. For whatever reason, she had to know how much pain I would take from her, and how much pain I could tolerate giving back. We were learning how to live "black and white together."

Breakfast in the Greene Street Church gave me a chance to explore the thinking of SCLC, when I found myself at the same table with Jim Bevel, one of Dr. King's strongest supports and an extremely charismatic leader in his own right. Jim, in characteristic style, welcomed conversation about SCLC and his own particular views, in the small group that clustered around him.

He told us that as far as SCLC was concerned, the battle for voting rights for blacks in the South was, to all intents and purposes, over. True, the Voting Rights Bill still had to pass Congress. But it was getting bipartisan support. There would be a difficult period ahead when blacks would be encouraged to register and vote. There was still the climactic march to Montgomery. For

SCLC that would be a showpiece; it would not change the irresistible forces now at work.

He predicted some violence and retaliation for SCLC's success. But the president's support of the Voting Rights Bill, coupled with black determination to see it through, would lead to revolutionary changes politically in the deep South.

What was SCLC's next step? Its leadership favored moving north, perhaps to New York City. In the same way that tackling voter rights in Alabama would help voter rights in all the other states, a concerted attack on the problems symbolized by the conditions in Harlem would point the way for the other big cities, north and south.

Bevel saw in New York City a power structure keeping the blacks in ghettos and underemployed, similar to the South, except that blacks in the North had the vote but had not learned to use it wisely.

When asked about current projects in New York like the East Harlem Protestant Parish and the current antipoverty programs, he thought they were well-intended but were "like trying to fight cancer with aspirin tablets. One must attack the problems, not the symptoms," he said. "One must get the people to demand a fair share of society's abundance."

"The SCLC is prepared to go to New York and, if necessary, bring the city to a complete standstill, with peaceful demonstrations such as we've seen in Selma, for solutions to the housing problem, the problem of police brutality, and of inadequate income for blacks and Puerto Ricans.

"We may not be economists," Bevel continued, "but we will certainly give the economists something to think about."

As a New Yorker, now picturing the same kind of marches through Wall Street that we had participated in on the streets of Selma, I wondered out loud if New York wasn't too huge, perhaps too bureaucratic and cold, incapable of changing its ways. He retorted, "All New York needs is twenty good preachers in Harlem." He cited Jim Orange as the kind of leader New York blacks needed.

Jim Orange was indeed an impressive figure as he participated in our demonstrations in Selma. A young man of huge physical proportions, he was immediately recognizable by the overalls he wore. Obviously from the farm, and without any formal education we were told, he nevertheless was a most gifted speaker. More than that, he radiated both leadership and goodwill. One wanted to hear him speak, or even just lead a freedom song.

One also sensed immediately how closely he related to the poor blacks of Alabama. He seemed to be in perpetual motion among the counties surrounding Selma, speaking in churches, meeting halls, homes, and open fields, at considerable risk to himself. And he was one of Dr. King's most trusted devotees of nonviolence, combined with a desire for justice. Bevel thought that a Jim Orange in New York could single-handedly stop gang fights, dope pushing, and delinquency. It was hard to argue the point. Jim Orange gave everybody hope, with his smile and his booming voice and his vision of how people could live together.

We returned to talking about the struggle in the South. Bevel challenged some of the deeply held views of his breakfast companions. I, for one, had assumed that the greatest physical danger to poor blacks in the South came from poor whites, the dispossessed, the lonely farmer, the so-called "poor white trash."

Not so, said Bevel. He posed that there is actually a bond of underlying sympathy, not often expressed, between poor whites and poor blacks, that the basic threat to the black comes from the well-organized middle and upper white classes. He maintained that the "nigger-haters" and the Klansmen drew their main support from the middle class. "When they are not involved in clandestine activities against blacks, they are serving on the boards of companies and sitting in the front rows of churches."

Put even more bluntly, the fact that President Johnson was federalizing the Alabama National Guard to protect the march to Montgomery, planned to begin in two days, had a two-way implication, as Bevel saw it. On the one hand the National Guard could protect us from others. And on the other hand, were they not in uniform "protecting" us, they might very well be the same men who would be sniping at us from the trees.

The power structure that held the black person down, according to Bevel, was very tightly knit. Whatever Governor Wallace said would most likely be taken as a cue to the rest of the white society. When the highest officers in government said that there would be no violence in a situation, or requested that there be no violence, there was no violence. But, if a high official described a situation as something they could not control, it was a signal to underlings to use terrorist methods, in the sure knowledge that they would not be prosecuted.

Bevel was convinced that when the church in Birmingham was bombed, killing the little girls, it was actually bombed by people in the state government. He admitted that no proof of the fact would stand up in court "because other people, of course, are arrested, and nothing can be proved against them because they didn't do it."

Breakfast over, I carried away one of his analogies: "Society is like a banquet table. Everybody has to bring something besides an appetite. However, society has structured itself so that the black person cannot make his contribution."

Following breakfast more groups were organized to visit the neighboring counties, and whites and blacks set off together.

In the afternoon a new tactic was devised—to send a sizeable group to picket Mayor Smitherman's home in an all-white neighborhood. His home was too far away to be reached by a march, so the picketers, men and women, got into a number of cars and headed toward his house. A few cars got close to the house. Others were intercepted along the way.

The would-be picketers discovered that they had aroused the ire of the white community in a way completely unmatched by previous demonstrations. The police pushed one group into a line roughly with their night sticks. Press and TV cameras were kept by the police at a distance, though a few press people slipped through the police line.

One policeman said, "You'll picket in front of the mayor's house over my dead body!" There was no question in anyone's mind but that he meant it.

The demonstrators were surprised to hear reporters describing events completely contrary to what was actually happening. If a policeman pushed a demonstrator, the reporter said in his microphone that the protester had pushed the policeman. It was reported to the outside world that protesters were hurling insults at the police, when in fact, the demonstrators were too frightened of the power being brought against them to think of aggravating it. It dawned on them that the press who had slipped through the police lines had been identified by the police as "friendly" press, people from not too far away, who could be "counted on" to give a proper interpretation of events.

Several other carloads of demonstrators were lined up and pushed against a wall outside a laundry, where fumes from the laundry were allowed to blow over them for more than two hours. They were then carried away in a wagon amid cursing and threats from the crowd that gathered. They tried singing "We Shall Overcome" in the wagon and were drowned out by deputies shouting "Shut up!"

Ultimately 315 would-be picketers found themselves being held in a Negro Neighborhood Center. Word got back to Carver Houses that they were under arrest. I began calling the families of the four Unitarian Universalist ministers being held: Rev. Arnold Thaw, Rev. Steve Graves, Rev. James Hobart, and Rev. Carl Ulrich.

It turned out that Commissioner Baker had not arrested the 315, but had put them in "protective custody," not wanting to give the added publicity through formal arrests. The "protective custody" turned out to be a misnomer, because early in the evening all the police left the group alone in the Neighborhood Center. They were free to go back to Sylvan Street. But since darkness had fallen, with its attendant dangers, they decided to spend the night in the center.

Several rabbis were among them. It was Friday night. So the rabbis were asked to lead everyone else in worship. This they did, assisted by non-Jews, in a service described later as both meaningful and beautiful. The rest of the evening was spent folk dancing. Early the next morning they came marching back on Sylvan Street amid the cheers of those who had seen them off the previous day.

Meanwhile, on Friday night there was another large mass meeting, without the 315 otherwise disposed. James Bevel was the principal speaker, and he amplified some of the remarks he had made at breakfast. He told us of his brief enrollment in a theological school, and how he had grown impatient speculating on what was going to happen in heaven. When he had given an unacceptable interpretation of Jesus' resurrection, he had been taken aside and encouraged "to return to the Dr. King crowd."

His humor savaged his seminary experience. "One of the favorite activities in the seminary was debating whether the Good Samaritan was a Negro or not. On the negative side of the argument is the fact that the Samaritan gave the wounded man wine — if he had been a Negro he would have killed the wine before he got there. But on the positive side of the argument was the fact that he left the man at the inn and said he'd pay later."

Bevel also recalled the days when the National Council of Churches wanted him to be a minister to migrant workers. "If I am their minister," he said to them, "I'll march them into the capital and stay there until they get a fair deal." Part of the program for migrant workers included giving each worker a little bag with a toothbrush in it and other small personal articles. Bevel had turned on his would-be employer and said, "That bag is going to take you right to hell."

Jim Bevel believed strongly in treating causes and not symptoms. One of the basic problems, as he saw it, was how to communicate with the white community. "White Selmans find it difficult to talk to monkeys. They are so fear-ridden that they turn off their TVs so they don't have to see the news, and pretend that nothing has happened. The white churches are completely ineffectual. They don't have enough preachers who believe strongly enough in what they say to live it. When most preachers preach, the people go home, eat a big dinner, and then go to sleep. If we can communicate, people will stay awake and start moving. It involves more than taking a stand. Everyone is taking a stand these days, and the result is that there is a lot of standing around.

"We ought to bring our missionaries back from Africa. They could tell these white folks that at least when the Africans kill a man, they're trying to get a meal. Every Saturday night at least twenty Negroes are killed in jail in Alabama. We must demonstrate that we want to participate in government and participate in society. The word on injustice must become flesh. We must be willing to die for hate-filled white children.

"We must go into the streets. Actually the Negroes have always been in the streets. When somebody asks, 'What do you want?' we should answer, 'What have you got?'"

The enemy for Bevel was the white power structure, which disenfranchised the black and kept him poor. "They complain about our stealing," he said. "The average income of Negroes in Selma is $1,800. If I only made $1,800 in a year, I'd steal too. When my back is hanging out and I know that Nelson Rockefeller has six hundred suits, I know that somebody stole my suit. We're ready to say to the white community that we're not going to live in shanties propped up with fishing poles while you walk off with all the money. We would like jobs, but we don't have to have jobs; we just want to share in the income that machines produce."

He concluded with the observation that white folks know too much and don't love enough, and that black people are ready now to handle the problems that whites have botched. "If love can be constructive in Dallas County where Clark is sheriff, it will work anywhere," he said.

I went to bed also pondering the words of an Episcopal bishop in Selma, that he was overcome with the power of love expressed in the Civil Rights movement. To the full assembly he said, "The church is too little and too late. But you people of color are going to renew the churches. The white people are enslaved. At this moment we whites ought simply to be quiet and listen."

Day Thirteen

Saturday, March 20. Following the return of the 315 from "protective custody," the morning was given to preparing for the march to Montgomery, scheduled to begin the following day.

Those hoping to walk the entire fifty miles were required to have a medical examination, provided by visiting doctors and nurses who always managed to be on the edges of the demonstrations. I passed my medical checkup by suppressing my hacking cough and not mentioning my numb toe to the doctor.

I telephoned my wife and told her that I hoped to be marching the fifty miles over the next five days, but that I planned to be home around Friday of next week. She informed me that she would be conducting the church school worship services on Sunday in my absence and leading the children especially in the singing of freedom songs, while I represented them in the heart of Dixie.

Back in Brown Chapel, procedures had been set up to determine who the three hundred fortunate people would be who could march all the way.

It was decided that only twenty-two people from outside the state would be permitted to be among the three hundred. All the others would be blacks drawn from Dallas, Greene, and Wilcox Counties. Among those 278 blacks priority would be given to persons who had been in jail or who had been beaten.

Seventy people applied to fill the twenty-two places for out-of-state marchers. A committee was set up to make a fair determination of who the twenty-two should be, with the thought that the twenty-two should be a representative group. I suddenly saw for the first time the possibility that I might not be able to march the full route.

When the list of twenty-two was finally posted, I was keenly disappointed not to find my name on it. Furthermore, somehow in the selection process no Unitarian Universalist was named. But I held in my hand the list of more than one hundred UU clergy alone who had passed through Selma since my arrival, and one of our ministers, James Reeb, had been killed in Selma.

Those on the list of twenty-two accepted tended to be the heads of national organizations such as labor unions. Many of them I recognized as recent arrivals in Selma. I resolved to bring to the committee the lack of representation of Unitarian Universalists.

I was making a second resolution to myself—that if I failed to make the final list the next day, I would make the march myself, in memory of Jim Reeb, and if necessary, following the three hundred marchers but without the protection of the federalized National Guard. It would be a dangerous thing to do, offering oneself almost as a target to an angry crowd. But I could not picture myself after the experiences of the previous thirteen days turning around one-fifth of the way to Montgomery.

When I spoke to the committee about the possible overlooking of the Unitarian Universalists and my unhappiness at not being considered to go the distance, I was corrected on the first point. Among the dozen or so marshals who would guide the marchers all the way, in special orange-red jackets and not counted among the twenty-two, would be a member of the Germantown Unitarian Church in Philadelphia, James Bell. He would be representing James Reeb.

Of course, this knowledge did not lessen my desire to make the fifty-mile march myself. When I said to one of the committee, "Maybe I'll just make the march myself, at the end of the procession," he came back with, "That sounds like you're putting yourself and your wishes ahead of everyone else's. Would you do it if it jeopardized everybody else?"

That, indeed, was a new thought for me and left me in a moral quandary that lasted more than twenty-four hours and through much of the next day's activity. I conceded to myself that standing on the line day and night the previous week vowing to go to Montgomery might have made me unreasonable on the subject of the march. I resolved to march as far as I could on the four-lane road, and then see if I could find some way to go on with the marchers.

In the early afternoon I managed two hours' sleep and returned to Brown Chapel just in time to see the Episcopalian contingent emerge from the chapel, only to be halted by

Commissioner Baker, and then hold a worship service on the steps of the chapel.

About 4:00 p.m. I went to our Unitarian Universalist "headquarters" to check on telephone messages. The TV in the living room was on, the family was watching, and clergy were crammed in all the available space cheering one side or the other of St. Johns University (NY) vs. Villanova (PA) in the final moments of the final game of the National Invitational Basketball Tournament. It was a marvelous diversion for all of us. Following the game a weatherman announced that it was snowing in New York.

About that time a long-distance call came for Morris Samuels, our Episcopal clergyman who had led us Sunday to the Episcopal church. He learned from the call that one of the three churches that he served in the Los Angeles area had been deliberately set afire and burned to the ground. Each of us thought of our churches back home and wondered whether danger lurked there as ominously as we had felt it in Selma.

Conversation among the ministers turned on various subjects. Before long we were discussing capital punishment with a minister from California who had once observed an execution. He told us that it was only necessary to watch a capital punishment once to know that it was wrong. He described how the witnesses and the press had been lined up and marched to the execution chamber in military formation. It was his opinion that doing things in a military way provided the dehumanizing atmosphere in which brutality could take place.

On returning to Sylvan Street I saw a boy triumphantly waving a Confederate flag. But this was a tin one, ripped off the front of a state trooper's car. Here was a real trophy, won with great valor in the middle of the night, it turned out. My first impulse was to ask him if he wished to sell it to me. Then I thought with some shame that I could undoubtedly give him enough money to buy it from him, but that it was rightfully his and not mine.

The evening mass meeting gave us more detailed instructions on how we were to behave on the march beginning the following day.

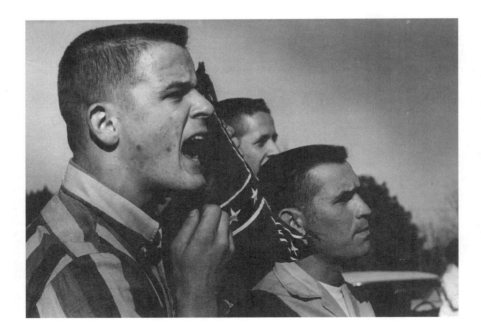

Photos©Ivan Massar

I slept from 1:30 to 6:00 a.m., knowing that I would march on Sunday, and hoping upon hope that somehow I could march the next four days as well.

Day Fourteen

Sunday, March 21. March 21—the day had arrived. People began assembling at the chapel as early as 6:00 a.m., prepared to make the march. From about 10:30 on, speeches were made from the chapel steps. The crowd continued to grow in size, while television cameras and newsmen swarmed over the block.

By 1:00 p.m. we were ready to leave. From my position near the chapel I looked back and saw something like six thousand people filling the street ten abreast into the distance, a sight one would never forget. Everything that I had brought to Selma I carried in my odd-looking travel bag, along with the parasol that had not been reclaimed by its owner. The soles of my shoes felt thin, and I noticed with dismay that a hole had already appeared in the left one. I decided to watch where I stepped and try to make the shoes last all the way to Montgomery.

We began to march. As I watched Brown Chapel receding behind me, I thought particularly of the several families that I had gotten to know so well and love. I wondered how long it would be before I would see them again, if ever, and what kind of reprisals might be in store for them once the huge procession had moved out of Selma. Had the great influx of visitors in fact been helpful to these courageous people? I was immediately sure that it had. One needed only to recall the warm enthusiasm that greeted every person coming into the community to know that it had given these people a tremendous boost in morale, and an elation that some people in the white folks' world cared enough for them to risk facing danger with them.

We swung down Water Street, on the same route we had followed almost two weeks earlier. I was sure we were passing the same people, now staring with wide-eyed amazement at the seemingly endless procession.

Already there were some ugly taunts coming at the marchers. Five feet ahead of me a man with only one leg marched briskly on crutches. I supposed that he would only go a short distance in the march. Almost immediately the angry whites on the sidelines singled him out as a target for abuse. "Boy, that will really make good copy in the newspaper," one said. And on three or four occasions that first day I heard small groups chanting, "Left, left, left, left" as he went by on his one leg.

Jim Letherer was from Saginaw, Michigan. I asked him later in the day if he was tired. Without answering my question, he looked me squarely in the eye and said, "You look a little tired yourself."

Once more we approached the Edmund Pettus Bridge. Could any of the marchers not have a huge lump in his or her throat while making the gradual climb? Down the other side, past the point of the March 7th beatings, past the point where we had been turned back two days later. We were now on the open road for Montgomery.

The National Guard was also now in evidence, spaced fairly regularly along the left-hand side of the road. Helicopters and airplanes buzzed overhead continuously. We marched in the extreme left-hand lane, and all the traffic on Route 80 passed back and forth on the other side of the island divider. Still, we were close enough to hear the gibes from both sides of the road.

While I was not much afraid of snipers, having been assured that all the snipers were in uniform that day "protecting" us, I did keep an eye out for rocks coming from either direction. No rocks were forthcoming, but we saw many Confederate flags and many angry people.

Cars passed on the road with signs painted on their sides, such as "Go home, white scum," and "Peace to Selma, Coonsville, U.S.A." The occupants of one car held up a sign reading, "Priests' Suits For Hire Here." In fact, the same cars kept appearing and reappearing on the road. It crossed my mind that they might all rendezvous when we made our encampment for the night.

At one point a group of older teenagers sat on the hood of a car very close to the line of march. One of them, obviously their leader, was yelling in an angry voice long before we could hear what he was saying. The press had gathered around him looking for a good story. As I passed, I heard him yell out, "Here's a press release for you. You can quote me as saying that Lyndon B. Johnson is a son of a bitch."

With many miles still to go, I reflected on something I had heard Jim Bevel say, namely, that the most dangerous whites in the community were not those of the lower class, the dispossessed, the poor farmers, and so on, but the middle- and upper-class young people, the ones who owned cars and whose fathers owned good portions of the town. I thought back on the angry young people I had seen, and it was true that they had all seemed quite well dressed, in fact, like college kids just home for a spring vacation, kids in sport clothes, driving their own cars.

How deep did this identification with the Confederacy really go? I recalled the story one white man had told me in Brown Chapel from his youth. He had grown up in Virginia. Fifty years after the Civil War was over, fighting continued between the sympathizers of the Confederacy and those of the Union. On a beach every day during the summer, the "rebels" would gather at one end and the "unions" at the other. At some point they would rush each other, swing and pummel and beat one another, and then withdraw. They didn't know the individuals with whom they were fighting or even understand the rationale for their behavior. I felt I was almost participating in a similar event, an acting out of Civil War history fed by primal human passions.

Our first day's hike was not to be a long one, seven miles in all. It seemed twice that long. We were glad to arrive at a huge field where many of us would spend the night. Four large tents had been pitched. People who had no intention of marching the whole fifty miles were getting into cars to head back to Selma or on to Montgomery.

The rest of us headed for the first tent. Each did the natural thing of staking out a small area where we might sleep. Our first meal on the road was a great success. I marveled at the system with which it was served, everything coming out of huge new galvanized garbage pails, and served piping hot.

By the time we had finished supper, everyone was ready to stretch out in the tents. Darkness had almost fallen by 8:00 p.m. But instead, there was a period of great confusion. A promised supply of air mattresses did not arrive; the generator failed occasionally, putting all the lights out. Everyone tried to find a suitable place to sleep.

Television cameras were also in the tent recording the scene. Eventually it must have dawned on somebody that pictures of boys and girls putting their sleeping bags alongside one another could be misinterpreted by the world at large or mishandled by a hostile press. So at that point the TV cameras were asked to leave the tent. The decision was made to separate the men from the women, the men going to another tent altogether. The third tent was being used by our security forces, and the fourth was reported to house supplies.

In fact, what we had begun to fear actually happened. The pictures taken in the tent at 8:00 p.m., of boys and girls putting their mattresses side by side, were used the next day in the Alabama legislature to illustrate the supposed rampant immorality in the camp.

I had difficulty getting to sleep as early as 9:00 p.m. There was a great deal of noise in the men's tent. When a huge portable heater misfired and filled the tent with acrid fumes, I left to get a breath of air. Returning to the tent later, I found my borrowed air mattress missing, appropriated apparently by someone without one. I decided to try sleeping on the ground, my head on my travel bag, and a raincoat and my ministerial robe as my protection from the cold. This did not work either. When my feet were thoroughly frozen, I left the tent to stand first by a fire someone had kindled in a metal oil drum, and then later by the generator itself, which was giving off a warm stream of air.

As I stood by the generator, others began collecting there also, simply to get warm. I fell into conversation with two young black women. I asked them if they were staying in the camp and, to my surprise, they said no, that they had driven out from Selma in order to see what it was like, and would soon be returning. I questioned their safety in making such a trip at that hour of the night.

One of the women opened her handbag toward me and I could see that it held a revolver. I asked quietly how that fit into the philosophy of the march, and she said that she made no claim to being a part of the nonviolent movement. As I thought of her and her companion driving back to Selma, I was not so sure that I could criticize her for "taking precautions."

A rumor had already circulated that a girl had been stabbed back in Selma. This rumor turned out to be unfounded.

In contemplating our security within the camp, there was some comfort in seeing the ring of fires burning brightly around the camp in the night, each one attended by a few National Guardsmen. Certainly it would have been difficult for anyone to slip through between the fires without being detected. On the other hand, the National Guardsmen were native white Alabamians. Up to this point they had shown us nothing but icy aloofness. In the event of trouble from the outside, could we be sure they would protect us?

The hours dragged by. The temperature was close to 32. I tried to keep warm by talking with several of the newsmen on the scene. They were an interesting lot, representing such papers as the Manchester *Guardian* and *Le Monde*. It was not easy to interpret to them what they had been witnessing in Alabama since they had arrived. They were looking for human interest stories as well, and as a now two-week veteran of the scene, I was able to provide some choice ones.

About 2:00 a.m., when the generator went dead again, I came to appreciate much more fully a young white man whose appearance was odd, to say the least. He wore glasses and had the bushiest beard I had ever seen. His rail-thin physique was enclosed in a suit of overalls. He moved easily back and forth among the pieces of machinery in the camp. In all, his appearance was not unlike the images of Jesus I had grown up with in a Protestant Sunday school.

I learned that his name was Tom Farr, that he was a native of, of all places, Canada, who had come to the southern tier of the United States with a kind of missionary zeal to help bring love to a troubled region. For the Selma campaign he had volunteered

94

to be the head of the "latrine detail," and also serve as a mechanic. His knowledge of mechanics proved to be of immense help to the marchers. During the five days of the march he seemed always to be at the right place at the right moment with a solution to a problem.

At 3:00 a.m., realizing that the generator was going to run out of gasoline before the sun came up, he took several people with him out to Route 80 and down the road to an all-night service station to bring back ten more gallons of gasoline to keep the sleepers warmer. I marveled at his bravery as he set out on foot at that hour. Later he told me that he earnestly looked forward to every encounter that he could have with a southern white person. In every encounter he felt he made a little progress in the easing of their fear of the Civil Rights movement.

At 3:30 I noticed that a seat in a nearby ambulance was not occupied. The driver was willing to let me sleep there for about an hour until he had to drive back to Selma. I spent two more hours in the sleeping bag of one of our own security men, Joe Nerad, while he was patrolling the camp. But with all my clothes on inside the sleeping bag, my feet simply refused to warm up.

It was a punishing night physically. The decision had not been made as to whether I would be able to march the fifty miles. If the answer tomorrow was yes, I would not regret this night.

Day Fifteen

Monday, March 22. The dawn finally came, and we prepared for Monday's leg of the journey, a total of seventeen miles to be covered that day. After breakfast I found that some of my Unitarian Universalist friends who had hoped to march the full fifty miles to Montgomery had found conditions in the camp too disheartening and were returning to Selma.

It was not much comfort when a truck drove into camp after breakfast containing blankets that we should have had the previous night. We were told that there had been some error in the shipment, and that the blankets had all gone to Boston by mistake, an irony for me since the headquarters of the Unitarian Universalist Association is in Boston.

Once on the road, we began to realize how far seventeen miles is when a thousand people not trained in the military try to move like a military unit. It reminded me somewhat of a family walking through a department store, with each member having a different pace and interests. Though keeping ranks, the marchers tended to move at slightly different speeds. The end result was exhaustion much sooner than if one were to walk the distance in a solo effort. Still, we had the singing to buoy our spirits, and there was no end of freedom songs to entertain us and to probably rile most of the onlookers by the road.

On passing Southside High School, we beheld something that brought tears to many of the marchers—an American flag flying directly in front of the school. After all of our experiences with the Confederate flag, the American flag looked like an outpost of civilization. Moreover, the children inside the school crowded their very white faces to the windows and actually waved to us, and called to us, and even cheered as we went by. I wondered what the history of the school was, and what their teacher was telling them or would tell them after we went past.

After the school, we were in open country, heading toward Lowndes County. Willow trees weighed down with Spanish moss dominated both sides of the road. We saw more and more swampland, reminding me of my vision of the Mississippi Delta. Helicopters and National Guardsmen were ever-present, while State Police cars raced back and forth on the road, perhaps trying to keep traffic moving.

When I saw a guardsman facing the swamp instead of facing us, while the other guardsmen continued to face us, it dawned on me that he alone was doing his duty. The guardsmen were there to "protect" us. Only he faced the direction from which danger might come. The others, while standing rigidly at parade rest, were either more interested in watching us, or thought we were the ones from whom violence might arise.

A bright red convertible car with Mississippi plates passed us with four blond coeds. To my complete amazement they were

96

singing from "We Shall Overcome" the verse "We are not afraid, we are not afraid, we are not afraid today, For deep in my heart, I do believe, we shall overcome one day." Thirty-two years later, my recollection of those four Mississippians remains almost an apparition.

A few miles farther down the road a dilapidated house was set far back from the highway. A black family was seated on the porch watching the parade go by. A National Guardsman stood where the highway met their driveway. The husband of the family had come exactly halfway down his long driveway and stood impassively watching the marchers go by, as erect as the guardsman, paying his cautious tribute to the movement.

Things seemed quite well-organized for the comfort of the marchers. Hertz and Avis rent-a-trucks were much in evidence, pulling the portable latrines to the head of the line of march. One had time to work one's way to the head of the column, enter a latrine, and come out again as the last of the marchers went past.

The rent-a-trucks also brought us our food. It occurred to me that the very presence of such nationally recognized organizations as Hertz and Avis was a big help to the Civil Rights movement, by simply representing an impartial national interest. I guessed that vehicles easily identified as belonging to the movement would not long remain on the road. I also wondered if Hertz had a service in hearses. The idea of a Hertz rent-a-hearse fascinated me for a time.

Sometime before lunch a small airplane passed overhead showering us with leaflets. The message of the leaflet was simple, if quite crudely written: Agitators would cease to agitate when they lost their jobs. This message was gratuitously given us by way of the "Smallest Air Force in the World," the Confederate Air Force, probably one plane. The airplane was not seen again during the five-day march.

We came to one National Guardsman standing alone at attention observing the march. I was surprised to see him smiling kindly on the whole procession. His was the first smile I had seen from a guardsman. Then I saw the star on his helmet. He was General Graham, in charge of the National Guard, and himself not an

Alabamian. I called out "Eyes Left!" and our part of the procession turned heads toward him and smiled back as we went by.

We passed through a crossroads town called Benton. As in previous towns it was the filling station attendants who looked-like they were ready to wade right into the procession with their fists. Some of the same cars we had seen the day before, with hostile slogans painted on them, were waiting for us in Benton. An overhanging sign read "Belcher's Service Station." It seemed more than appropriate.

I had noticed how white onlookers, for the most part, stayed a great distance from us, often almost hiding behind their cars as they watched us go by. I even looked to see if they were behind trees and wondered if we could possibly be such an awesome sight. Then we would come upon a group of blacks crowding the road, cheering us, throwing kisses, and looking as though they probably would be joining us at the end of the procession.

I fell into conversation from time to time with my old friend whom I had come to call "Big Bear," the boy who had taken me to the black restaurant on my third day in Selma, where I had not stayed to eat. At one point he said to me on the march, "When I go back to jail, they'll keep me there this time, and I'll get a good whuppin'."

Later I talked with one of the marshals, in his orange-red jacket. He was also a white minister. He said that when he told his father on the telephone that he was in Selma, Alabama, with the protesters, his father told him he hoped he'd get shot.

By 11:00 a.m. we could see the end of the four-lane highway. The difficult moment had come, that of paring the marchers from the now 450 persons down to the 300, which were all we were permitted by the federal ruling. Those who had not marched all the way thus far were asked first to step out of rank. Then those who would volunteer could step aside. I was not ready to give up my spot.

The remainder were sorted into smaller groups, those from Dallas County, those from Greene County, those from Wilcox and Lowndes Counties. There was even a group who had come that far knowing they were alternates to the twenty-two out-of-state whites. A few had dropped out from the original twenty-two, but their places had been filled.

However, by now some of the marshals recognized my intense desire to complete the trip. Moreover, mine was a familiar face to almost everyone, blacks and whites, from standing at the Selma Wall for so many hours, and being present in Selma as long or longer than any of the twenty-two other whites. They offered to make me a marshal if necessary, so that I could continue the march.

The offer to be a marshal did not thrill me, because of the awkward bag I was carrying, the holes developing in both of my shoes, and my generally tired and run-down condition that had me sometimes almost running at the end of the procession just to not get left behind to what I imagined were the howling wolves of segregation. I said I would be a marshal if that were the only way for me to continue. Committee heads huddled. An announcement was made that the number of whites participating was being upped from twenty-two to twenty-five. I was in. My elation at being among the "select" was enormous.

We now embarked on the two-lane highway through Lowndes County, which one native had described in the chapel as having "more kooks to the square inch than any other place in the world." Lowndes County was one of the few counties in Alabama that had registered no blacks for voting. It claimed not even to have had one voting application from a black person in eighty-six years.

The fact that we were on a two-lane road meant that we would march in the left lane and that the fairly heavy traffic on Route 80 would have to be controlled by the State Police moving a line of cars first in the one direction and then a line in the other direction. The cars passed very close to us for the next several days, and we were able to look at their license plates and the faces in the windows, a fascinating study for me that helped to pass the time.

For instance, a truckload of Mexican farmhands passed, and we exchanged wild greetings. A car from Maine went by, and the elderly couple were painfully unhappy at finding themselves a part of history. Many people gave us sympathetic waves, and one or two whom we expected to be sympathetic stuck out their tongues or hurled obscenities.

When we would stop for a fifteen-minute break, as we did from time to time, I found that I could sit down, put my head on my arms, and fall fast asleep. When I was awakened, it seemed as though I had slept for several hours instead of fifteen minutes.

We finally arrived at our campsite for the night. I was grateful that the night was warmer than the previous one. A short mass meeting was held and everybody turned in again about 8:00 p.m. I was not quite ready to sleep at that hour and lingered outside the tent.

One of our security people came to me and whispered, "Would you like some orange juice?" That was almost like saying, "Would you like a pot of gold delivered to you every week?" I whispered back that I would. We sneaked off to a car where he revealed a milk bottle full of orange juice, and we each had a glassful. Because it was done so secretively, I had a gnawing feeling that I was doing something quite wrong, like engaging in a black market operation.

Several days later, when I heard that the Alabama legislature was concerned about "immorality" in our camp, there was a mention of clergy supposedly drinking liquor. I saw no evidence of liquor in my four nights around the camp. But I could not help wondering whether a newsman had happened to see two of us slip away to drink orange juice and thought we were enjoying alcohol on the sly.

At each encampment there were always a few beer cans lying in the field when we entered. The clean-up crew tried to leave each camp unlittered the next morning, but may have missed a few cans. The story of heavy drinking at the campsites was completely unjustified, I believe—people had their hearts set on only one goal, getting to Montgomery.

That evening I realized for the first time that the march was traveling with a portable radio station. When we pitched our tents at the end of a march, a fifteen-foot antenna was raised alongside the communications vehicle. I learned that the station was operated by the Student Nonviolent Coordinating

Committee on a short-wave frequency approved by the Federal Communications Commission. SNCC maintained stations in Montgomery, Birmingham, and other points, and kept a continual flow of information passing around among their various headquarters. Though recognized as a sympathizer, I was not permitted in the truck to watch the station in operation.

That night I managed four and a half hours of sleep since the tent was much quieter than the one the previous night. I also had the luxury of a blanket to wrap around my otherwise icy feet.

About 3:30 a.m. I was awakened by what sounded like a shot. I left the tent to ask about it. Somebody else said he thought he had heard four shots. However, there was no more excitement, and there was never any record of violence that night.

I stood by the fire and was surprised to hear a minister whom I had met earlier in the day talking very loudly and rather incoherently about theology to someone who was obviously not interested in the slightest. Later I learned that one of the ministers had to be withdrawn from the march the next morning. I assumed it was the same person, cracking under the emotional strain of events.

Unable to go back to sleep, I patrolled the area for a while. In the very early morning my heart stopped when I went around a corner of the tent in the dark and met a person coming at me who looked every inch an Apache warrior, his face heavily painted. It seems that he had put on sunburn cream during the day and had just not bothered to take it off at night. Draped with a blanket over his shoulder, his appearance was enough to throw anyone in the camp into panic.

Day Sixteen

Tuesday, March 23. Just as we finished breakfast, we were greeted with a cold drizzle from the heavens. Then, as we broke camp, the rain came down harder, then very hard indeed.

I was one of only a few with an umbrella, though many had hats. After a while I was wet enough, even with a raincoat and a clerical robe, that the umbrella didn't make much difference, so

I closed it up. It was a cold day, too. Holes had appeared in the soles of both my shoes. I could feel the water sloshing back and forth in them as we began the day's eleven-mile hike.

About the only thing to break the monotony of marching through that dreary county on that dreary day were the freedom songs that we sang that never really ended. The same song could be sung for half an hour, with people continually inventing new verses, to which the rest of us would respond in chorus. As usual, we included Governor Wallace, Sheriff Clark, Commissioner Baker, Mayor Smitherman, and Al Lingo in our love chants.

Mid-morning a truck drove by from which oranges were thrown to the marchers. Oranges still tasted better to me in Alabama than any other food.

Later we passed a field of jet black cows. All appeared to be marching resolutely in the same direction that we were, toward Montgomery. They were roundly cheered. The singing continued, with verses about the cows. The rain kept up unabated. Many cars drove past us containing blacks who were too frightened even to look out their windows at the passing parade.

I mentioned casually to one of the marshals that several nights before I had actually seen a revolver in the camp, thought it was not owned by a marcher. He responded that he would not be too surprised if among the three hundred marchers ten revolvers might be found among them. This shocked me, since I had come to think that everyone marching with us was completely wedded to the idea of nonviolence. However, having an idea of the number of firearms that were arrayed against us all along the way, and knowing that our guns could never possibly be used except if we were attacked, I found that I did get a small degree of comfort in knowing that we were not completely defenseless.

I pondered how deeply committed I was to the ideal of nonviolence. The more I thought about it along the many miles of march that day, the more I knew that I had personally been converted completely to it. At the same time, I wanted to understand the fear that prompted others to carry weapons.

We ate our lunch in the rain, and we marched in the rain through the early afternoon. The worst was yet ahead of us.

When we arrived at our campsite, the tents were up. But the field was a complete quagmire, with mud deep enough to ooze over the tops of our shoes. Nor was it much drier under the tents, because it had been raining long before the tents were pitched. A liberal supply of hay had been brought in and laid both inside the tents and out. But the mud was too deep. The hay very quickly became wet and sank into the mud, sometimes out of sight. I was rapidly reaching the most depressed moment for me in my 18 days in the South; I was too tired to stand any longer, and there was just no place to even sit down, much less lie down.

I finally found a small patch of relatively dry hay outside the tent and sat down on it, resting my head on my arms and dozing off immediately. A few minutes later I was toppling over in the mud, and I righted myself. Again I put my head on my arms. Then I was aware of a rather violent quarrel going on near me between two photographers. It seemed that they were jockeying for position near me. I saw that they each wanted to get the better picture of me when I toppled over into the mud again. Since I did not particularly want to appear in *Life* magazine with my face in the mud, I stood up and moved to another place and left them to find some other object for their cameras.

A man went sloshing past, muttering half aloud that this was worse than New Guinea in 1944. The Unitarian serving on our security forces, James Bell, confided to me that our security had gone "completely to smash," and that nobody knew what he or she was doing at that point.

But things began to look up. The rain stopped at last. It was rumored that we had new celebrities in camp, including Pernell Roberts and his wife. Pernell Roberts played the part of Adam in the popular TV show *Bonanza*. I managed to talk to the two of them for fifteen or twenty minutes and got his autograph for each of my daughters, knowing that this would make my absence from home almost justified in their eyes.

Air mattresses were handed out. Mine turned out to be leaking air and not very comfortable. But at least it was something to sit on to separate me from the mud.

An American flag had been planted on a small incline over-looking the road in front of our tent. It looked so good to me that I put my mattress down close to it and spent many minutes just contemplating it.

As night closed in, I took off my mud-caked shoes and wet socks and hoped upon hope that it would not rain during the night. I slept from about 8:00 p.m. until about 1:30 a.m., when I was awakened by peals of thunder and flashes of lightning. How-ever, the storm passed slightly to the north, and we got no more rain that night.

I dozed off several more times, and each time had a night-mare. In one I was back in Selma and the whole project was overrun by thousands of state troopers. I was caught with my notes on me, the notes that I had been writing whenever I found a moment during the 18 days. Needless to say, in actuality I had taken great care all along the line to make sure that they were not on me when I was liable for arrest, and that I was never separat-ed from them on the five-day march.

As I sat on my air mattress and looked out on the sea of mud, and realized that I would eventually have to climb back into cold, wet socks and barely recognizable shoes, open at the soles and caked with mud, for another fifteen-mile walk, perhaps in the rain, I had no trouble identifying with Job in the Old Testa-ment sitting on his dung heap and asking why he was born.

At 4:30 a.m. I was struck by how very, very dark the sky was. I found myself singing softly the hymn "Oh God, Our Help in Ages Past," including especially the verse "Short as the watch that ends the night before the rising sun."

By 5:00 a.m. the sky was getting light.

Day Seventeen

Wednesday, March 24. The first announcement of the morning from the communications truck was that the water we had been drinking on the march had been found to be unfit. We were asked to empty our canteens and fill them with water from an army truck that had come into the camp. I had not carried a canteen. I had consumed large quantities of the "unfit" water along the way, which had had the flavor and smell of kerosene. (I did not hear of anyone subsequently becoming sick from our first supply of water.)

By 7:00 a.m. I had forced the wet shoes and socks onto cold and aching feet. Breakfast was completed; we were ready to march. Montgomery was only a day and a half away, and we were eager to put the mud pit behind us and be on the road again.

As the march resumed, we were greeted almost immediately by a big black man hanging out of a car window shouting, "I don't know you, you bastards!" A few minutes later a car drove by with a white woman screaming at the top of her lungs, "The South shall rise again!"

The National Guardsmen presented a new picture to us; word had come from a higher authority during the night that they were there to protect us, not to stare at us. Now, to a man, they faced away from us looking into the menacing woods and swamps.

While we marched I learned that on the previous night one of the guardsmen had spit on a priest, but that the guardsman had immediately been relieved of his post by his superior.

At last in the distance we could see the place where the highway opened up again into four lanes. We would no longer be bound to the limit of three hundred marchers. And we could see what looked like hordes of people, friendly people, cheering our arrival, anxious to join in the march. They had come in the very early morning from both Selma and Montgomery. The procession quickly swelled to a thousand people and kept growing.

Buses and cars kept coming toward us along the highway from Montgomery as we marched. They emptied out their cleanly scrubbed passengers, who first loudly cheered and greeted us, then took up positions in the march. I began to see familiar faces from my church in New York. Each was a huge surprise to me, and I could feel my body heat returning from the excitement.

For the first time I took stock of the gruesome appearance I was presenting as their minister. For several days I had been unable to get a comb through my matted hair and had given up any attempt in that direction. The beard, hacked off at such a furious pace in New York, was getting its revenge by its spotty and ragged reappearance. I had not changed my shirt in three days, although a clean one was in my travel bag; there had been no place to change into it without freezing or getting the new shirt immediately soaked with water.

The marching itself was more difficult for me than on previous days because of the condition of my legs and shoes. I frequently found myself at the tail end of the procession struggling to keep up. A temptation arose to drop the parasol by the wayside, as a stricken plane might jettison fuel, but I remembered the faces of the mother and her little boy as they had urged it upon me. The sun was hot that morning. Everyone, including light-skinned blacks, was getting sunburned.

Then, for a change of pace, it poured hard again in the early afternoon. The newly scrubbed were getting their baptism.

But we were definitely coming into Montgomery. Houses were closer together. More people were jeering and cheering. Among the billboards by the road was a large one in red, white, and blue with the message, "Help get the United States out of the United Nations," with an address and telephone number for those who wished to join the movement.

We were continually heartened to hear of the great numbers of people still arriving in Montgomery to join the final leg of the march the next day to the capitol. It was reported that a whole trainload of people had gotten as far as Atlanta, but had had to switch to buses to get to Montgomery when the crew of the train walked off.

I fell into conversation with a young black girl from Selma who had early in the march taken a particular liking to me and insisted on marching with me much of the way. She was fourteen years old, the middle child in a family of eleven children. Her father had died some years before, and her mother was on welfare and receiving Social Security checks. The older children, by and large, had gone to other cities to live and "settle down."

At fourteen, this young woman had been arrested four times, the last time with a group of clergypeople near the mayor's house

106

on the previous Friday. I asked her why she had gone along on that particular trip. She said that she had never seen the mayor's house, or any part of the "place where white folks live," for that matter, and she was curious just to see it.

She aimed to be a psychologist when she was grown. She had qualified for the three hundred marchers because she had been part of the group that crossed the Pettus Bridge on March 7th. A heavily applied nightstick had left her sore for several days, but she had not had to go to the hospital.

In mid-afternoon we arrived in the suburb of St. Jude, actually a Roman Catholic parish serving blacks in the outskirts of Montgomery. By this time we were being cheered wildly by people on both sides of the street. One could imagine how veterans returning from a foreign war might feel, in our time or in Caesar's. Our songs grew firmer; our step had more snap to it. Jim Letherer, the one-legged marcher from Saginaw, was still marching, having gone the entire distance with the exception of several steep hills.

By now the procession numbered close to ten thousand persons. And almost all of them marched onto the prepared campground at St. Jude's School and Hospital. Because of the rain we were once more bogged down in mud.

One look at mud three or four inches deep convinced me that I could not face another night of sleeping in it if there was any alternative to be had. I toyed with the idea and finally decided to attempt to get into a hotel in Montgomery where I had learned some of our Unitarian Universalist clergy were staying preparing for tomorrow. I assumed that there would be room for me on someone's floor at least and an opportunity to take a bath.

Going into town now would mean that I would miss the gala performance that had been arranged for tonight in the campsite, with a host of top-notch performers headed by Harry Belafonte; Peter, Paul and Mary; Odetta; and Joan Baez. But my desire to get out of the mud dominated me. I was joined by another UU just arrived, Alison Mathews, who was serving as a correspondent for a newspaper. We decided that we would try to make the trip into Montgomery together and make sure we were back tomorrow in time to make the remaining march to the capitol.

As we got to the main gate at St. Jude's, it was just being closed, as a security precaution and in an effort to control traffic around the compound. Plead as we did, we were told we would have to slog another quarter of a mile through the mud to another gate even to leave the site.

So we slipped and slid in the mud another quarter of a mile and came to a place where cars were discharging and picking up people. I looked for a taxi, with a black driver, of course, but did not see one.

Before us, however, was a car with a very pleasant-looking black couple in the front seats. I asked them if there was any possibility that they could drive us to the Jefferson Davis Hotel, where my friends were staying. They replied that they would be glad to do it if we did not mind stopping at their house first. Alison and I of course were in no hurry, so we gratefully accepted their offer.

The couple drove us about half a mile to their home. By then they had proposed that I take a bath at their place, change shirts and clean up my shoes before walking into the Jefferson Davis, one of Montgomery's better hotels.

Once in their home, the thought struck me that hardwood floors are basically the same everywhere for sleeping, and that there was no need for me to go downtown if I could just sleep on their floor, any floor, for the night. As tactfully as I could, I put this possibility before them.

They replied that they would be delighted to have Alison and me as their guests for the night. Before I could head for the bathtub, they had pressed a can of cold beer in my hand, which, after drinking water flavored with kerosene (or was it kerosene flavored with water?), could not have tasted better. Out came a second beer. Thus fortified, I climbed into the tub, cleaned myself as I had never scrubbed before, washed out my matted hair, put on clean clothes, and reemerged feeling like an entirely different person.

To my amazement, my host had used the time to graciously clean my shoes and provide me with a fresh pair of his own socks. My shoes literally sparkled on the topside, though the holes in the soles remained.

Dinner followed, consisting of barbecued chicken and other treats. By the time dinner was over, I felt that the world was beautiful and that the state of Alabama had some very bright spots indeed.

Our hostess, by now undoubtedly inspired by the transformation she had affected in me, was busy on the telephone arranging for other guests to come to their house to spend the night, and for whole busloads of people to be farmed out into their community for hospitality. Because I had fortuitously stumbled upon a couple with obvious standing in their community, I was not completely surprised when in the front door walked A. D. King, Martin Luther King Jr.'s brother. Introductions were made all the way around, and I was grateful that he had not seen me in my previous condition of disrepair.

Six of us visited in the living room for a while. I wanted very much to hear the others' perspectives on the Civil Rights movement and what they thought of the march. But try as I might, I could not fight off some long-overdue sleep, and I feel asleep in my chair.

Mercifully, I was shown to a bedroom. I expected to sleep on the floor and consider myself lucky. Instead I was shown a lovely bed with its covers turned down, waiting for me. Whose bed it was I didn't ask or care. I was asleep before 8:00 p.m., while A. D. King held forth in the living room and Odetta; Peter, Paul and Mary; and others undoubtedly were "doing their thing" on the improvised outdoor stage at St. Jude's Parish.

Day Eighteen

Thursday, March 25. At 6:00 a.m. I was gradually waking up. I was conscious of a very loud noise, which I thought at first was the roar of the generator at a campsite, since the little bit of sleep

I had gotten on previous nights was near the generator I had attempted to take advantage of for the small amount of heat it threw off.

But I was also aware that now I was sleeping in a bed, and I was very, very warm. I finally investigated the noise and found that it was somebody snoring in the other bed in the room. The snorer turned out to be A. D. King.

Though I was the first person up, our host and hostess immediately arose and served a wonderful breakfast before taking some of us back to St. Jude's to resume the march. They also let me call my family in New York to tell them that I would probably be home that night or the next day.

At St. Jude's I found that the bright orange jackets worn by the marshals on the march had been given out the previous night to the three hundred marchers who had gone the fifty miles. But they had run out of jackets before all the marchers had gotten theirs. I was naturally determined to obtain one of the jackets, if possible. When a fresh supply came in, I was first in line, and I donned mine with great pride.

Once more there was a hubbub of activity as the thousands of marchers prepared for the final four miles into the capital. One boy was walking through the mud in his stocking feet complaining that somebody had borrowed his shoes and failed to return them. Every car within the gates of the compound had bogged down in the mud and had to be pushed out by willing volunteers.

People were collecting signatures from their friends, knowing that they might not see them again for a long time, if ever. The fourteen-year-old girl who had marched with me much of the way signed my jacket and I signed hers and others', as requested. "Big Bear" also signed mine.

I saw one more young man whose signature I wanted on my jacket, a teenager who had been with us on the line and at all the meetings and had made the long trek from Selma. When I asked him to put his name on my jacket, he told me sheepishly that he didn't know how to write his name. "But I can write *freedom*," he said. "Then write *freedom*," I said, and he carefully spelled it out on my jacket. I put his name alongside it.

One of the marshals whom I had gotten to know well in five days went past. I noticed how badly swollen and cracked his lips were from the weather. He told me about the previous night's "gala performance," which I had missed, how they had tried to pitch a tent to house it, but the tent had collapsed. So it had been held outdoors on a wooden platform. The platform was so small that all the entertainers had to crowd together, along with the press, who fought for positions for getting pictures. The public address system was not as good as it should have been at the beginning, and everybody of the thousands present kept pressing forward toward the platform in order to hear better. Those who were caught next to the platform were lucky that their limbs were not broken, or worse.

But it had been a great performance, all agreed. At one point Odetta was standing on the edge of the platform waiting for her turn to sing and rubbed her shoulder as if it were sore. My friend had jumped up and asked her if she wanted a back rub, and she had said it would be heaven. So for half an hour he gave her a shoulder massage before her turn to sing. It was the high point of his evening.

As we lined up to march this morning, my attention went to a row of very good-looking girls, black and white, with different colored sweatshirts, all bearing the insignia of Mundelein College. I had to ask them where Mundelein College was, and they told me that it is in Chicago. It consisted of twelve hundred girls; twenty-three of them had come to Montgomery to march. They added color to an already colorful procession. Many banners and hundreds of American flags were being distributed.

About 11:00 a.m. we began to march the last four miles. At first the route passed through the black section of the city. Almost to a person, the people on the sidelines cheered us on, despite the endless procession.

Then we were in the downtown area marching past the bigger hotels. There were some whites on the street, but most of the whites had followed George Wallace's instruction to stay away from the line of march. A few hung out of hotel windows and thumbed their noses at us.

Proudly we marched through the center of Confederate Square, in the cradle of the Confederacy, toward the capitol building six blocks ahead. The line now was ten or twelve abreast and more than a half-mile long. Those of us with the orange jackets, the fifty-mile marchers, were supposed to be in the lead directly behind Dr. King. But in fact, everybody was crowding forward, jockeying for position in order to get close to the capitol steps and the rostrum. Those of us with orange jackets were lost in the crowd.

A block from the capitol we passed the Dexter Avenue Baptist Church, which Dr. King was serving at the time that he instituted the Montgomery bus boycott.

Then we were at the capitol, a building of immense beauty, for us marred only by the fact that at the top of its dome flew only the flags of Alabama and the Confederacy. The fifty-mile marchers were invited to sit as a group before the rostrum and for the next twenty minutes, as the rest of the marchers moved into position, we were entertained by last night's performers—Peter, Paul and Mary; Harry Belafonte; Joan Baez; and others.

The formal program began at 1:00 p.m. with the singing of "The Star Spangled Banner." Hundreds of American flags waved behind us. The possemen in front of us on the capitol steps did not remove their helmets. A group of Alabama legislators stood behind the sheriff's men as a kind of informal reception committee. During the next two hours of speeches and songs, they smirked and talked among themselves without ceasing, as if to drown out the voices of our country's ambassador to the United Nations and Dr. King himself.

By now I was too weary or emotionally drained to record the many speeches of the afternoon. But I was aware that I was part of a unique historical moment in world history. As Dr. King had said that morning, in one sense "we had overcome," just by our presence in Montgomery in such numbers.

Mrs. Rosa Parks was introduced and stood up, described by Dr. King as "The First Lady of the Movement" because of her unwillingess to surrender her seat to a white man on a Montgomery bus almost ten years before. Dr. Ralph Bunche, our U.N. ambassador, referred to the members of the movement as the "contemporary Minute Men of American freedom."

Albert Turner spoke. Albert Turner was a black from Marion in Wilcox County, where intimidation of blacks was said to have been greater than it had been even in Selma. Yet he had continually been in the forefront of the movement pressing for voting rights. He and Rev. Hosea Williams had led the fateful march across the bridge on March 7th. Now he stood on the capitol steps and courageously spelled out in detail how blacks had been prevented from voting in Wilcox County. His words were within earshot of the governor. Certainly some of the legislators and the armed force of the state could hear. I wondered how such a man could survive in the days ahead when the marchers had returned to their distant homes.

Lastly, I settled back to hear the slow, familiar drone of Martin Luther King as he very carefully and clearly traced the history of the freedom movement in the South like a skillful lawyer who knows he has a convincing case. Finally he intoned, "How long, O Lord, how long, before we will have our freedom?" and then answered, "Soon!" With his famous measured cadence he built up to his final words, a repeat from the Montgomery bus boycott, "Our feets are tired, but our souls are rested." Many of us shouted, "Amen."

A petition that had been drafted to be given to Governor Wallace was read to the assemblage, which resoundingly voted its approval. A committee to deliver the petition was also announced and accepted. We concluded the program with yet another singing of "We Shall Overcome."

With that, the pilgrimage was over. As the estimated thirty-five to forty thousand people slowly dispersed in all directions, I felt more than a little lost. I had an airplane ticket back to New York in my pocket, but no reservation and no way even to get to the Montgomery Airport. An expected ride to Atlanta did not develop. I finally walked several blocks to where a vast crowd was assembling to be carried in buses to the airport.

There, literally hundreds of clergypeople, many of whom had arrived in Montgomery within the past twenty-four hours, perhaps to walk the last four miles or just cross the street from their hotel, anxiously looked at their watches and jockeyed with one another to get in position to board the empty buses as they drove up.

I was still wearing my orange jacket that showed I had marched fifty miles, but no one particularly knew or cared what the orange jacket represented. After missing two or three buses and watching the clergymen struggling amongst themselves, I spotted a young man on crutches who had been equally unable to board a bus. I told him that if he would follow me, I would see that he got on the next bus. As the bus drove up, I told all the clergypeople in my loudest and most authoritative voice to stand back and let this young man get on next. He got on next, and I was right behind him.

I sat down behind the driver. As the crowded bus pulled away, I felt more like talking to him than I did to the church people, some of whom were talking theology or making fun of the freedom songs by singing outlandish words to them. The driver, white and a native Alabamian, turned out to be an exceedingly nice fellow and apparently was completely in sympathy with our demonstration.

When we disembarked at the airport, it was a far different scene than the one I had witnessed on my arrival seventeen days before. The airport was completely overrun with civil rights people, who sprawled out on the grass, filled the waiting room, waited at the restaurant, and lined up at the ticket windows hoping for transportation that night. The Delta Airlines representative told me that the first available space on their flights was two days away. Eastern Airlines, on the other hand, was putting on extra flights and was happy to exchange my Delta ticket for a flight leaving for Atlanta in several hours.

There was still business to conduct. One airplane, just in from Denver, had brought many boxes of food designated for the community in Selma. There was a problem of where to stack this food and how to get it to Selma. With a little time before my flight I made several unsuccessful telephone calls to try to work on the problem. Then I spotted Andrew Young, one of Dr. King's young leaders of SCLC. He promised to have the food picked up. Several of us stacked it almost on the curb at the airport entrance and took turns guarding it.

Hungry rights workers tried to buy the food from us, particularly the oranges, until they learned where the food was destined. While someone else guarded the food, I walked to the footlocker where I had deposited $150 seventeen days earlier. I had entrusted the locker key to a minister heading back to New York many days earlier. Now I couldn't remember which minister I had given the key to. Perhaps the $150 still sat in the locker a few inches from my grasp. It seemed a small price to have paid for the "Selma experience."

On my last tour guarding the food before I had to leave for my plane, an ambulance sped past, its sirens going full blast. It was on Route 80, our march route, heading for Selma. I hardly paid attention to it. Only on arriving in New York did I learn of the shooting and death of Mrs. Viola Liuzzo at that hour. Then I knew where the ambulance had been headed. Mrs. Liuzzo had brought her car from Detroit to help transport people and supplies in the cause. I wondered if she had been coming to pick up the food that I guarded.

The plane lifted off the runway at 10:05 p.m. Even as the runway began to fall away from us, I thought with relief, "I'm out of Alabama."

Four businessmen across the aisle flirted with a stewardess and then were quite upset that there was no deck of cards on the plane with which they might play bridge. I was moving back into the real world.

Landing in Atlanta, it seemed like another country from Montgomery. The airport that had felt so cold and unfriendly on the way to Selma now was festive and warm. Airline personnel smoothly made my ticket over to a United Airlines flight leaving almost immediately. I was surprised on boarding to find the plane less than filled. I took an aisle seat in the second row. I then was more than surprised when the seats in the row ahead of me were occupied by Joan Baez and two of her friends.

This time, as we headed down the runway, I bade farewell to Dixie, at least for now. I began to doze off, even as Joan Baez took her famous guitar out of its case and began to croon in her even more famous voice over the public address system to those who could stay awake.

I couldn't. With her foot on my chair to support her guitar, she sang to us for the entire three-hour flight to New York. When I awoke in New York, I felt tremendous gratitude that she had sung to all of us for those hours, with her face so close to mine that I could have reached out and touched her, and great regret that I hadn't really heard a single song she sang.

Walking across the terminal floor at 3:00 in the morning, I was more alone than I could ever remember. Ahead of me lay my family and my church, eager to welcome me back. Behind me lay a community of which I will always feel a part.

At that moment I was not only alone but also feeling the same terror that being alone in Alabama would have raised in me. I hesitated to get into a taxi by myself with a white driver who might lecture to me for thirty miles on the folly of the March to Montgomery.

Then I saw that my driver was a smiling black man. My fear evaporated.

Memories of Selma

About five hundred Unitarian Universalists participated in the 1965 voting rights demonstrations in Selma and Montgomery, Alabama. Among them were more than one hundred Unitarian Universalist ministers. More than thirty years later, in 1999, Rev. Jack Mendelsohn and Judith Frediani began soliciting first-hand accounts from Unitarian Universalists who were there. In the months that followed their request, Mendelsohn and Frediani received an outpouring of responses in many forms—memoirs, journals, personal correspondence, sermons, and published articles. As it turned out, there were too many individuals who still remembered vividly those crucial days in Selma. Although the responses were too numerous and lengthy to include here in their entirety, selections appear on the following pages.

We were late, very late, twelve years late. The first voter registration drive was in 1952. They were beaten into submission, beaten on street corners, on the steps of the courthouse, in their own churches, in their own homes—and we did not notice. Nor all the intervening years, punctuated by places: Nashville, Montgomery, Birmingham. They discomfited us only slightly. Nor did we notice that January 2nd of 1965 saw a new voter registration drive in Selma. The days and their freight of brutality, or unjust arrests, of imprisonment without right of counsel, or even of communication, of inhuman treatment, nights in jail without cover, cattle prodders, vicious beatings, and the death of Jimmy Lee Jackson in a nearby town. These things we did not notice, to our shame.

—*David A. Johnson*

Knowing all, we have still *done* little. We have done little about Boston. We have done little about Selma. We know the facts about Selma, and hundreds of other places. We could take up the crusade against their injustices with less fear of reprisal than those who live there, and yet we remain silent.

—*Gordon Gibson*

My children were watching television that awful Sunday afternoon. One of them came to the living room where I was reading the paper and said, "Dad, you had better see this!" There, in vivid and stark imagery, were "storm troopers" clubbing and trampling a bunch of mostly local citizens. The group was only trying to walk over the Pettus Bridge, an action intended to reach Montgomery, Alabama, there to petition the legislature to redress the cruelty and wickedness of then extant anti-black laws and racist customs. Presently the phone rang. It was Brad Greeley. (Brad was chaplain for the Concord Academy, and I was minister of the First Parish in Concord, Massachusetts.) His question: Shall we go? We assured one another: We must. And so we did.

—*Arthur Jellis*

The Social Action Committee of our church, augmented by board members, met at 8:00 p.m. last Monday night. The events of Sunday in Selma, Alabama, made all other subjects irrelevant. The question posed was twofold. Should we be represented in Alabama—physically present in the person of one of us—and would the committee guarantee the expenses of whoever might go. By 10:45 p.m. I was packing, packing only what was necessary—leaving behind all that I feared to lose—wondering what lay ahead that long night and the day to follow.

—David A. Johnson

After witnessing the Selma violence on TV, I was trying to figure out what could be done by my concerned friends and myself when a call came offering me three alternatives: (1) go to Montgomery that evening, (2) pay for someone else to go, and (3) take care of someone's children to free them to go. This call came through the UUA office, I'm sure. I talked it over with my husband, and we decided that because of the danger just one of us should go. And I chose to do it.

—Grace Linquist

When the secretary of the Central Midwest District relayed Dr. King's call to me on Monday, March 8th, I said I would join other Chicago clergy of all faiths on that 2:00 a.m. flight to Montgomery. Perhaps going as a group lent courage to a coward. Would we have gone alone?

—Hunter Leggitt

I had no money for the airline tickets, and no credit card either. A parishioner, Stan Blonski, who had a store in downtown Hamilton, literally emptied his till for me.

—Robert Hemstreet

I was living in Atlanta with my husband and three small children. My husband (probably wisely, but not to my liking then) said he didn't think I should go because of the children. I scoured the house for blankets—sent off as many as I could, and rued staying home. I understand my husband's concern, but I'm still sorry I didn't go.

—*Elizabeth McMaster*

A call came from the minister of the Mt. Vernon Church, John Wells, that he had been asked by Martin Luther King Jr. to send down people to give support to the march. It would not take many guesses to know who would go. Her thunderstruck husband found his objections unavailing. She [Judy Street] was going and that was that. To his astonishment, he found this gentle creature, who abhorred camping even under a tent, moving off down the train platform with nothing more than a rolled-up blanket, leaving Tom and the two teenage boys staring forlornly through the bars as all they held most dearly in the world moved determinedly toward an unknown and possibly terminal fate.

—*Greg Street*

I thought I was going primarily to observe. Orloff Miller, who was a close friend, seemed to pick up the fact that I was taking this all too lightly. I remember vividly that he told me, "Don't go to Selma unless it is more important that you go than that you come back." I think it may have been after that that Judy and I made our wills, a sobering thing at the age of 25.

—*Gordon Gibson*

Entering Alabama

Through the small hours we drove. Every town in Georgia seemed blessed with at least one police car. We painfully observed the speed limits, wondering how the police felt about outside agitators—particularly when one police car followed us briefly. Sometime before dawn we entered Alabama. We saw no signs until we reached Montgomery. The roads were hardly marked at all. We felt as though we were playing a deadly game and the other side had the only rulebook. As we approached

Montgomery, the signs didn't say "city limits" but, more ominously, "Montgomery Police Jurisdiction." We passed through quickly. On the other side of Montgomery the parking lot of a large motel was filled with at least 150 State Police cars. We were later to joke about the enemy resting for battle while we drove through the night, but it didn't seem humorous then.

—David A. Johnson

The ride from Birmingham was the first inkling I got of the world into which I had jumped. We rode in a big old sedan, windows wide in the warm day with two blacks who were part of the volunteer corps shuttling folks to Selma. The pickup trucks that passed us with rebel flags flying and unfriendly white faces peering at us woke me to the reality of being in the deep South.

—W. Bradford Greeley

As we traveled along the Jefferson Davis Highway toward the city of Selma, on that first morning, I saw a sign saying, "Christ died for the ungodly." Later that week I was to wonder many times just who the ungodly were, and how the sacrifice of Christ, who died unresisting, might be efficacious in melting the stone-like hearts of officialdom caught in a posture of ungodliness.

—Ford Lewis

Going to Selma was a kind of "going home" for me because I had lived and worked in Selma only six years earlier. I was a social worker in a child care agency living in the white community and knowing nothing of a black community. It soon became apparent in 1965 following my arrival in Selma that this "going home" was not what I might have been expecting. Participants in the Selma civil rights activity were unwelcome in the white community, and members of our group who attempted to walk through the community were arrested and jailed. Visiting a former place of employment was considered unacceptable.

—Una Joyce Williams

When I stopped for coffee and close conversation with some Hudson High students in a black cafe in an alley, a couple of determined-looking black men appeared and sat near the door, presumably guarding against trouble. While this looked like any other American city, it was difficult for me to realize how dangerous it was for a Northerner just to be there.

—*Gerry Bailey*

A man just asked me: "Why are you here?" Why am I here? I have three sons. I just discovered that their backyard bordered on a police state.

—*Richard Norsworthy*

I learned by seeing with my own eyes that the state of Alabama does not really consider itself a part of the United States of America. On the flag staff rising from the dome of the capitol was first of all a Confederate flag, and then a state flag, no American flag in sight! The state troops who had been federalized were wearing a Confederate insignia on their uniforms— not a United States emblem!

—*Helen Dick*

Selma was strictly segregated living, with all the blacks in one part of town and all the whites in the other. I knew and expected that. But I wasn't prepared for the abrupt change in the street when you crossed the line—the white side was paved while on the black side you were ankle deep in mud. When we finally marched under court order, we soon were outside the town. Along the road were shacks where the black people lived—with the families often out front waving to us as we went by. I grew up on a hog farm in Ohio where we would have been appalled to have had hogs as ill-housed as those people were. Back off the highway were the beautiful plantation houses that reminded me of Tara in the film version of *Gone With the Wind*. The stark contrast between the affluence of whites and the poverty of blacks was a picture worth a thousand words.

—*Edwin A. Lane*

One cold, clear morning Rudy Nemser and I took a walk in the black housing area on the edge of Selma. A vast sea of shacks extended as far as you could see over a flat, poorly drained area. The March rains had turned the unpaved streets into a quagmire. There were no curbs or sidewalks, and muddy ruts moved in and out among the homes in a crazy fashion. Crooked porch railings and roof supports and wobbly fences. No parallel lines like Northern suburbs. Occasionally there would be a chimney standing alone. Residents called the Selma firemen chimney savers, because that was all that was left by the time they arrived at one of their homes ablaze.

— *Gerry Bailey*

If I had never known what poverty was like, it came forcefully to my attention one day when I went walking in the downtown area. A black accompanied me, calling my attention to something happening in the alleyway we were passing. A barrel in the alley was at the back door of a grocery store. It was filled with scraps of meat and other waste. I watched as a mother lifted the cover and brought up from inside the barrel food which she took away. My companion suggested I go down the alleyway and take a look into the waste barrel. I did and when lifting the cover looked down into the barrel at a moving blanket of maggots.

— *Theodore A. Webb*

I spend most of one day working with Hunter Leggitt, a Unitarian minister from New York, arranging housing for our people in the project, and I get a chance to talk with the beautiful people, who are sharing what little food they have and their beds with people they've never seen before, and will probably never see again. In one house there is a man who is raising ten kids in five rooms, and there are six ministers sleeping in there too. They sleep in shifts. Everywhere there are roaches, and that's because the city of Selma never gets around to taking care of the project.

— *Robert Hohler*

The hospitality of the families of Brown Chapel and the broader black community in Selma was generous and welcoming to all the visitors. The numbers were many. The spirit of the community —adults, children, and youth—was embracing and caring. They provided community organization, housing, and food for the visitors and everyone marched, played, and sang together for the cause of civil rights. The opportunity to live out that hope for togetherness across racial, religious, and socioeconomic lines and to do it with inclusiveness was a lesson on possibilities for the future.

—Una Joyce Williams

There were many hundreds of people in that neighborhood around the churches and around the apartments in the project. The teenagers were like teenagers everywhere, playing, teasing, taunting, talking their own special language, wearing their funny clothes. But happy and knowing that they were participating in something vital, that something was going on in which they had a part and that they could give their living witness for an ideal shared by all races, all faiths, all ages, and shared as human beings. Little children would come to us after they had come to know us, and take us by the hand just as naturally as our own children might have done.

—Ford Lewis

The "compound" surrounding Brown's Chapel resembled a revival meeting and dinner on the grounds, but it was much more: It was a loving community. It was absolutely infectious. Those marvelous people, most of whom lived on three thousand dollars a year or less, opened their homes, their refrigerators, and their hearts to us privileged whites because we were of one mind and purpose that day.

—Charles Blackburn

I learned in Selma that interest in civil rights and brotherhood is not confined to any sect. The Roman Catholics were there, nuns, priests, and laymen, Negro and white. Jews, of course, were there, both rabbis and congregants, as well as various Protestant denominations. Among those gathered there, there was a sense of common destiny, expressed with power by Dr. King when he said, "We are caught in a single network of mutuality, tied in a single garment of destiny."

—Ford Lewis

For the first time in my life—I was thirty-six—I had an intense conversation with a nun (from Detroit), coming away knowing her as a human being with feelings and concerns. "I never felt so cloistered in all my life," she said. "One day in Selma is worth five years of maturity." She was not that remote figure in a strange "penguin suit," which was all I had previously known of nuns.

—Edwin A. Lane

On our first evening in Selma, we gathered in the Brown Chapel, where people from near and far, from all walks of life, and of every religious affiliation, spoke of their reasons for coming to Selma. And then for well over an hour there was a great outburst of freedom songs and hymns. And finally for fifteen minutes or more we sang nothing but "amens." The "amens" somehow expressed our need to go beyond words.

—Irene K. Murdock

"NEVER HAVE I HEARD SUCH SINGING!"

What intrigues me most of all is the line on Sylvan Street. Stretched across one side are Wilson Baker's city police, Jim Clark's possemen, and Al Lingo's troopers. They are armed to the teeth, and they stand there row after row after row. On the other side of the barricade are anywhere from a hundred to a thousand people, depending on the hour, and they are singing and preaching to the troopers, the possemen, and the police. This has been going on for a hundred hours, and no matter what time it is, you can always hear the singing and always see the line. When night falls, the cops turn on spotlights and head-lights, and it is a gorgeous sight. They've made up songs about Selma and they sing them to the troopers, and they stamp their feet and clap their hands, and nobody feels tired, except maybe the troopers.

—*Robert Hohler*

The room to which I was assigned had a window overlooking a makeshift wooden barrier in the road. A policeman stood on one side of the barrier; a few representative would-be marchers on our side. Maybe it was because I was exhausted from the trip or the anxiety; whatever, I slept well that first night. After that night there was always a small group of us at the barrier singing freedom songs. The singing went on all day and all night. Years later, when I heard any of the songs, the memories brought tears to my eyes.

—*Ralph Stutzman*

Everything is touch and go in Selma. The singing of freedom songs saves the day when tension gets high. Never have I heard such singing!

—*Howard G. Matson*

"We Shall Overcome" was very powerful. The phrase "We are not afraid" really worked. We sang this verse louder than the rest.

—*Grace Linquist*

I saw in Selma how an entire group of people constituting more than a majority of the citizens of that city were able to pray and sing their way out of despondency and transcend depression and gather courage and vitality and momentum to themselves and their movement. They sang such songs as one that contains the verse "If you look for me in the back of the bus and don't find me nowhere, come on up to the front of the bus, I'll be sittin' up there."

—*Ford Lewis*

A young SNCC worker is speaking. "I hope we're gonna make up our minds that if anyone gets whupped out there today, it ain't gonna be our women." Then he and another boy, not more than seventeen, demonstrate the ways in which we can throw our bodies over a woman who has been struck down by a trooper and how we can offer our backs and shoulders to their clubs. I see Methodist Bishop John Wesley Lord of Washington, D.C. He is standing in the aisle craning his neck to get a good look. Bishop Lord is in front of three women also from Washington — Mrs. Charles Tobey, Mrs. Harold Ickes, and Mrs. Paul Douglas. These three could just as well have been awaiting the invocation of the good bishop prior to beginning a luncheon of Washington wives but for the reality represented by the two kids in front of them. And Willie Bolden, the older of the boys, his face marked by short jagged scars, says to us in a weary voice, "There ain't no perfect way of showing you how not to get hurt. The only way I know is not to go."

— Robert Hohler

I could have been shot, or beaten, or killed. It was quite possible, but it was more likely that I would spend a few days here and I would sing freedom songs and join protest marches. And I would be proud to stand up and be counted and offer my presence to bear witness. And then I would leave that terrible scene with its frightening atmosphere and go home safely. But these people who lived here had to endure this awful struggle day after day, and little children were growing up in constant fear and terror.

— Irene K. Murdock

We will probably always deny the immediacy of unpleasant challenges. In that sense we are sinful, being less sensitive to wrong when it is injuring our brother than when it is injuring us. That means that Negroes are going to have to be the leaders in the struggle for rights and human decency. They are the ones who are oppressed, who cannot retreat from this battle, because they are the battleground.

—*Gordon Gibson*

I have never witnessed such calmness, ease, compassion, and grace in men whose living is a constant threat of death. It may be that if we whites are ever saved—saved from our lethargy—we will be saved by the Negro.

—*David A. Johnson*

A young man of about fifteen years of age lived in the apartment in which I was billeted. His head had a bandage that covered over half his face and head. Present in that first group that marched over the bridge, he and everyone else ran and scrambled when the State Police attacked. A young girl in front of him fell. He threw his body over hers to protect her as a trooper on horseback rode over him, the horse's hoof kicking his head.

—*Ralph Stutzman*

I was tremendously affected by the words and actions of both the SNCC and SCLC staff and many of the local people. It was a tremendous fusing of love and justice into action. My theology has been permanently affected.

—*Gordon Gibson*

It took our Unitarian ministers but a short time to become aware that they were but students in the hands of a most gifted Negro leadership. For example, when we went out on a demonstration confronting the police at a particularly ugly moment, Rev. Vivian advised avoiding physical contact, but on the other hand advised making the confrontation creative. "Meet them face to face, person to person, eye to eye," he said. When someone asked if we should not recite the Lord's Prayer, Vivian replied, "Don't you think that would be too repetitive and mechanical?

Would it not be better to say a friendly word like 'God bless you' or 'Peace be with you'?"

—*Howard G. Matson*

One remembers Bill Greer, an SCLC leader, who went without sleep or food for three days and nights when the other leaders were in Montgomery in court—who almost never lost his temper, who kept us on several occasions from acting foolishly and perhaps violently. The SNCC worker, a veteran of three years in Mississippi, who has been beaten and dry shaved and jailed, who tells you, "Man, I only make ten dollars a week, but I'm a free cat."

—*Hunter Leggitt*

The night King arrived, I was ill, tired. When King came into the crowded chapel, a thousand people jammed in it. It was dark and chilly, and then I saw him, and it was like the scene in *Henry V*: "Now let us entertain conjectures of a time when creeping murmur and the pouring dark fills the wide vessel of the universe," and his presence—this unsmiling, patient, quiet man—shone, like Henry, "with a largess universal, like the sun."

—*Clarke Dewey Wells*

We might think that because the black people have been so grievously discriminated against and disenfranchised they would be ready to adopt some other philosophy or political ideology. I spoke about this with my host, Mr. James Durry. He said, "No, I'm not interested in any other ideology. At least here I can struggle and someone will help me." I felt warm. We were slow enough in coming, but nevertheless we were there at last trying to help.

—*Ford Lewis*

The overtones and nuances of freedom as it exists in the movement extend far beyond the gaining of legal rights for one minority, essential as that is. The meaning of the movement reaches to every town, city, or crossroads where men and women live unfree. The movement, ages and ages hence, may redeem community and create a world where people no longer look out of their apartment windows while others are being beaten in the streets below. "Because most people's consciences are moved when other people's bodies are battered," as C. T. Vivian told us, the movement shall overcome.

—*Hunter Leggitt*

It is the hope and aim of such leaders as Dr. King not only to gain civil and political rights for Negroes, but to gain a new humanity for all Americans, black and white. Their aim is not to humiliate the white Southerner, but to win him over. Of course this is a difficult process. As James Baldwin has pointed out, it ironically demands of those members of society who have been most deprived and most injured that they be the best trained and the least vindictive. From the standpoint of logic this makes no sense, but from the standpoint of human dynamics it makes superb and magnificent sense and is working.

—*Gordon Gibson*

Frequently I heard, among the many lofty utterances that I was privileged to hear and able to jot down, people testifying of their determination "to tell the truth with their bodies." One was reminded, of course, of the injunction of Paul to present our bodies as a living sacrifice on behalf of our principles and our beliefs. And that is exactly what people in the Southern Christian Leadership Conference movement have been doing for ten years, telling the truth with their bodies. They have been walking in an orderly and restrained and inoffensive way up to the very face of the entrenched opposition and have been saying in strength but with love, and in the spirit of nonviolence, "We want to tell the truth about life with our bodies. If necessary, with our lives."

—*Ford Lewis*

"Every Time I Saw a Police Car I Flinched"

Believe me, no man or woman or child can stand eyeball to eyeball with a state trooper swinging a homemade bludgeon, its center filled with lead, with a lethal crushing power, this trooper swinging it on the end of a leather thong as he stares at you with hating, frightened eyes—and as you walk up to him, he turns to the trooper next to him and remarks, "You get him [meaning me] and I'll take the Sister [meaning the nun who was next to me]"—no one can do this without knowing in the pit of your whole being that you have just offered your bare and defenseless body as a witness to the truth.

—*Hunter Leggitt*

Fear? Yes, in the stomach, throat, knees; pulsating in my eyes; pounding in the head. I had grown up believing the police to be my protectorate, my friends. My days and nights in Selma proved so traumatic that, once back home on Long Island, for months every time I saw a police car I flinched.

—*Ralph Stutzman*

If you want to go to throw bricks and pop bottles at Jim Clark—stay home. If you fear you will answer hatred with hatred—stay home, for they preach no hatred in Brown Chapel. If you go, take no halfhearted commitment, for there is no place for it in Selma. Take your life with you as a gift entire—for just to be there is a risk of everything you are or hope to be. You will find the terror unbearable if you go in any other spirit.

—*David A. Johnson*

I learned many things about myself during the Selma experience. One was that I am a natural born coward. On each plane trip to the South, I asked myself why I was doing this. I had voting rights. My state did not refuse to register blacks. And I had to overcome my fears by realizing over and over again that all people suffer when our democracy hurts any part of its people. Again, on the march, I figured that the end of the line was the

132

safest place to be, but as I tried to be last in line, I discovered others had determined the same thing, and I found myself being edged toward the front.

—David H. Cole

As I sat in that dirty Selma jail by way of punishment, I was possessed by two feelings: (1) fear, not knowing what was going to happen to me next in that dark jail—but (2) certainty that I was doing what was right and that I didn't want to be anywhere else.

—Arnold Thaw

We were kept in the courtroom overnight, the jail being already full. We were visited by a black clergyman and three people from the local Jewish synagogue. It happened to be the Jewish holiday of Purim, and they brought scrolls for the rabbis to use in the Purim ritual. Purim commemorates the time Esther intervened with the king on behalf of the oppressed Jews of Persia. The courtroom was transformed into a synagogue as the rabbis conducted the solemn ritual. It was an observance that had special meaning for all of us in that courtroom that night.

—David H. Cole

You have heard about the days in the county jail and unheated Camp Selma. You have heard about the toilet that was constantly getting stopped up, about men and women in their seventies and eighties forced to sleep on cold concrete floors while mattresses and blankets were stacked just outside the door. You have heard about the one tub of water, our sole source for washing *and* drinking. I think that in the response of this and other groups of prisoners one can find the essence and meaning of the freedom movement. All of us, I think, had low moments and complained some, but very few complained chronically. Instead, we accepted the conditions almost joyfully. If *they* could inflict it, *we* could take it, for unearned suffering is indeed redemptive.

—Gordon Gibson

Our feet, our bodies were now involved, fear and all. At least, and at last, we now knew some of the terror African Americans had been living with all their lives. For many clergy, Selma, Alabama, had become a turning point.

—*Ralph Stutzman*

There was a great deal of criticism of King's decision to proceed on a "morality above law" basis. What was not generally recognized was that most of the participants in that march were aware of the consequences of breaking the law and were prepared to take those consequences, a significant factor of responsible behavior and decision making that was not comprehended fully nor communicated in the media.

—*Charles Blackburn*

A few withdrew, reluctantly. They felt that defying the federal court was unjustified and counterproductive. I knew what they were feeling. Yet all around were others like Homer Jack and Bob Jones of the UUA Washington office, for whom the question paled before the basic issue. For me this became a critical moment when my whole life hung in the balance. Here stood Martin Luther King, the greatest modern American exemplar of what I said I believed. Would I follow, or hang back? We had seen what these police were prepared to do. Billy sticks at the ready, they now waited in close order at the approach to Pettus Bridge. Against this, there was no question of the rightness of the cause we supported. I decided to go, and with a strange tranquility took a place not far from the front of the line wending its way toward the river.

—*Walter Royal Jones Sr.*

The bridge is deserted and I think for a while that they're going to let us march to Montgomery. Then I look back and I see the State Police pulling in cars behind the end of the line and I reach the crest of the narrow bridge and look down the road to see a solid phalanx of troopers blocking the way and possemen lining each side of it. I am walking beside an elderly black

134

woman who says to me, "This is where they threw the tear gas Sunday." "Were you on the march?" "Yeah," she says, "I've been on eight of them." We are marching into this box of troopers and possemen and I don't see any way out of it. I ask her, "Where did you go when they threw the bombs?" She says, "You take my hand. I know the place real well."

—Robert Hohler

I was in the tenth or so rank. A graying, small lady was on my left. To be in that procession was frightening and unnerving action. I did neither weep nor tremble—or so I thought. But my marching partner knew it was bad going for me. She reached over the short distance between us, took my hand, and said, "We're going to be all right." And it was so.

—Arthur Jellis

We're told to stand and to link arms and we sing "We Shall Overcome," and I think, OK, this is it. Here we go. But no, instead I hear a ripple of applause behind me and as I turn to look I see Farley Wheelwright walk by with Emily Taft Douglas on one arm and Mrs. Charles Tobey on the other. On they go to the head of the line and I wonder will they hit the wife of a senator over the head? I'm sure the trooper beside me would, if he got a chance. Then the word comes down the line that we're turning around and I see some of the SNCC kids with their bedrolls walking back and they're crying.

—Robert Hohler

THE ATTACK ON REEB, OLSEN AND MILLER

Word reached us minutes later at Brown Chapel and thus began a night of terror. Rumors flew that the ambulance had broken down, that it had been followed, that the men would never get there. We called the FBI and asked for an escort for it. It never appeared. I hurried to the Negro infirmary and discovered that the ambulance had gotten a flat tire and three cars of whites had stopped by it and peppered its occupants with menacing questions. One man had to be restrained from beating the driver. A police car had come up and the policeman had asked equally hostile questions and refused them an escort—not the last to refuse them, for a state trooper refused them later, saying brusquely, "You don't need one."

—*David A. Johnson*

Ever since that day I have thought of the few moments Arthur and I spent talking to Clark Olsen and Orloff Miller and a guy named Jim Reeb on the way to dinner. They said they knew of a place on Main Street, but we declined to go with them and found a local spot in the black part of Selma where we were spending the night. I can't imagine how life might have been different if we had gone along with them.

—*W. Bradford Greeley*

When we returned to Washington, the national television cameras greeted us. I reported having dinner with Jim and how three of our group had turned right and the rest went to the left upon leaving the restaurant in Selma, and remarked, "There but for the grace of God would be me." This was the first my mother and father in Boston knew of my involvement and, needless to say, they were not happy.

—*David H. Cole*

At 8:00 p.m. we learned from Birmingham that Jim Reeb was dead. Our weariness fell more heavily upon us. We were all tired, desperately tired; the weight of anxiety, the pressure of time, the anger at incomprehensible cruelty, the frustration of uncompletedness, the fear of the always present possibility of violence—all had eaten into us and corroded our spirits. The time had come for me to leave, and I wanted to go home. But what shall we say of those whose home is Selma, whose life is born in poverty, bred on insult and indignity, nourished on fear, encompassed by frustration, and limited by every structure of society. For them, Selma is home.

—*David A. Johnson*

Jim's death galvanized the nation—a nation that had hardly noticed a few days before when Jimmy Lee Jackson, a local Negro, had been shot and killed during a similar demonstration —but James Reeb was a white minister from the North, and President Johnson sent yellow roses to his hospital room and called him "that good man."

—Orloff W. Miller

Another man died in Selma, within the same social context, shot by a state trooper in an atmosphere of violence. Jimmy Lee Jackson was a human being in his own eyes, in the eyes of his mother, in the eyes of his grandmother, and in the eyes of those who were a part of his life. They loved him and they miss him, just as James Reeb is missed by his family.

—Lawrence McGinty

The profound sympathetic reactions of President Lyndon Johnson and most of the people in this land were difficult to comprehend for those of us so caught up in the immediacy of the tragedy. The twisted minds of the arch-segregationists were so stunned at the wave of revulsion that they lashed out that Jim was a plant, an intentional martyr; a sick but somewhat understandable reaction as glimpses of Jim's life as a minister in a ghetto in Boston were revealed by the news media. There were many gains as a result of the Selma events, but one of the tragedies was that white America was unable to feel the death of Jimmy Lee Jackson with the same intensity as that of Jim Reeb.

—Charles Blackburn

Then as many as can jam inside that small church for a memorial service for Jim Reeb, and there are Unitarian and Universalists inside and outside, and I feel like Eliot Richardson, who said, "Our grief is tempered only by our pride."

—Robert Hohler

Walter Reuther, as we stood before the courthouse in Selma memorializing Jim Reeb, told us, and I think truly, that Jim Reeb would not have us hate those who struck him down, for he would say, "We were trying to save them, too."

— Ford Lewis

MARCH TO MONTGOMERY, MARCH 21–25

We were instructed to stay with a buddy, to march with groups of six, not to speak or wave to whites, not to drop out of line, to ignore remarks, to have men march on the outside of the lines.

— Grace Linquist

Standing in the mud. Back aches. Feet numb. 8:30 in the morning. In Montgomery. At of all places the City of Saint Jude. The Catholic saint of the impossible. And it all does seem impossible. The girl beside me is from Canada, British Columbia. What in hell is she doing here? What in hell am I doing here? What is anybody doing in this lousy playground sunk in the gray mud of Alabama? We're moving out, somebody says. Everybody straightens up. We link arms and move forward about five feet and stop. We stand there linked together for a few minutes and finally drop apart when it appears we're not going any farther.

— Robert Hohler

Finally, as we marched we saw people sitting on porches and at curbs. We saw cripples, invalids, school children waving and smiling. We saw some kindergartners lined up singing ". . . and before I'll be a slave . . ." to the white community, with people on porches or at windows, just staring. Some spat on and insulted marchers. Singing helped to relieve our tension. I remember clearly that I had never seen hate stares in my life and felt so sad and sorry for those people.

— Grace Linquist

We are holding on to one another for dear life, singing at the top of our lungs and then shouting, "one man, one vote." Pernell Roberts is in front of us with his wife. He looks as if he just came off the set from *Bonanza,* and he's got this American flag all furled up, and the Canadian girl grabs it and helps him unfurl it, and we are marching like the Union Infantry up the hill to the spot where Jefferson Davis was sworn in as the president of the Confederacy. Flying over Confederate headquarters are the stars and bars. All around us people are producing American flags, and the first thing somebody says after we all get there is, "Let's sing the National Anthem," and if I were Otto Preminger and this were a movie set, this is probably the way I would stage it, because we begin to sing and the sun comes out and the wind begins to flow and the flags begin to wave in the breeze. It is all very cornball. But I have trouble seeing because of the tears in my eyes, and I step on a guy who is stretched out on the ground. It turns out he's a Unitarian from Maryland and he is saying the same thing that has been ringing in my ears for days now: "It can't stop here."

—Robert Hohler

The final day we all marched into Montgomery, singing and holding hands while being cursed at and spat upon by hate-filled crowds along the road. Never in my life had I experienced such feverishly hopeful and hostile emotion jammed together until that day I strode alongside sisters and brothers into Montgomery, trying, as Andy Young exhorted us, "to love the hell out of Alabama!"

—Tom Owen-Towle

Now King is on the platform and he is saying that we have come up a highway from darkness. And I'm thinking maybe my road has not been to Montgomery, but to Damascus, and that maybe a lot of us had to come to Alabama to find redemption. Maybe a lot of Unitarians and Universalists have found something on those muddy Alabama streets that has been missing from their lives for too long a time.

— *Robert Hohler*

Suddenly, it was all over. A public announcement was made over the loudspeaker: "The National Guard is disbanding. There are no local police. Go back to the railroad station immediately; walk on the main streets; don't take side streets. Don't stop to buy anything—and *do* stick together."

— *Judy Hodson Street*

As I stood in front of Brown Chapel waiting for my ride to the airport, I was sad but quietly at peace. The afternoon sun was bright and I felt its warmth throughout my body. I felt unified with the motley assortment of people who were standing, talking, or moving about in the helter-skelter fashion so typical of this. How did anything get accomplished in this craziness, I marveled, but proudly knew.

— *Gerry Bailey*

LOOKING BACK

In the late seventies, early eighties, I became aware of a son of Viola Liuzzo's. I asked him whether he would be our guest preacher on Easter morning in memory and in honor of Viola Liuzzo. In essence, what he said was that his mother was never adequately honored because she was a woman and people said, "Why did she not stay with her five kids instead of running off to Selma?" Meanwhile male civil rights workers were lionized as heroes. He told the tale of his family, how crosses were burned on their lawn after Viola's death, how his father's hair, almost overnight, turned from black to white, how he and his siblings were beaten up at school as "nigger lovers."

— *Rudi Gelsey*

Friday evening, March 26th, my picture appeared on the front page of the *Huntsville Times* carrying the Huntsville sign in the Selma-Montgomery march. That night the church was stoned. Many of the windows in the church school were shattered. Then the phone calls began: 250 of them before we got an unlisted number. Some were threatening; most were obscene. In rapid succession, the New Orleans Unitarian Church was bombed; the UU minister in Jackson, Mississippi, was shot; the Birmingham church was guarded twenty-four hours a day after a bomb threat. The Klan reorganized in Huntsville and held a meeting in a field near our house. We placed heavy wire mesh screens over the windows and floodlights on each corner of the house and examined the car for bombs every morning before starting up.

—Charles Blackburn

We are the ones who go and they are the ones who remain. The unspoken question is what happens to them when the whites leave. As I left, a Negro lady said to me, "It was nice to have you. I hope you can visit again." She made it sound as though I had made a social call. Neither of us talked about what might happen when we left.

—Howard G. Matson

How can a man ever forget what it meant to be in Selma the week of March 7th, 1965? If I could give each of you just one gift for a lifetime, it would be to have spent that week in Selma. Those of us who were in Selma will have to do as Jim Bevel urged us to do: retire into our closets and rethink our entire philosophy of life. No less is possible.

—Hunter Leggitt

My final memory is of the parade held in Concord shortly after we returned. What was most noticeable and powerful was the attitude of the police. Arthur and I found ourselves greeting them and thanking them as we walked along. We were thankful beyond measure to be living in a world where we did not have to fear the wrath of the police along with everything else.

—*W. Bradford Greeley*

When I went to Selma, and then to Montgomery, I felt shame and sadness, fear and humiliation, and finally, a deep commitment to work to make my religion real on behalf of all people who seek and deserve "freedom now." Street demonstrations, boycotts, and civil disobedience should no longer be necessary to rouse us to the need for action for civil rights.

—*Connie Burgess*

Whereas before I believed in honesty and fairness, my faith in enforcement of the law was badly shaken. Life was not fair. Middle-class virtue was meaningless in the face of poverty, repression, and despair. The essential goodness and worth of humanity overcame all competing values. It was people that really counted. You don't have to be or do anything to qualify for consideration. The abstract principles had melted away in favor of a warming sense of humanity that aligned all my values and gave meaning and purpose to my existence.

—*Gerry Bailey*

I opened a dusty storage box and began reading from a foot-thick file of clippings and looking at pictures of bombed-out churches and peaceful demonstrators being bludgeoned to unconsciousness. A vortex of emotions ensued: depression, elation, pain, and poignancy. Memories of commitment and terror shook me as I relived those days of tragedy and triumph in the Civil Rights movement in the South.

—*Charles Blackburn*

I joined in the crusade in one town in one state, for two weeks, and people thought I was somehow courageous and exemplary. I was not. Were I to live up to my professed ideals, I would have stayed there; I would not have withdrawn from the battle until it was won.

— Gordon Gibson

For me, Selma was a high point, an unforgettable experience, but for all of us it is an historical time, never to be forgotten. We have come a long way, but there is still much to be done, and it sometimes seems we take one step forward and then two steps backward. The struggle goes on. "Eternal vigilance is the price of liberty," said one of our great patriots. May we hold fast to our dreams and be eternally vigilant in order that the battle may one day be truly and rightfully won.

— Irene K. Murdock

Answering the Call

The following is a list of Unitarian Universalist ministers known to have participated in the voting rights demonstrations in Selma and Montgomery, Alabama, in 1965. This list was compiled from information given by those who were there and participants' families.

Adams, Eugene H.

Anderson, Francis C. Jr.

Arisian, Khoren Jr.

Beebe, Lawrence E.

Blackburn, Charles B.

Botermans, Karel F.

Blalock, Ira J.

Botley, Robert D.

Bowman, Robert M.

Bridges, Gene

Brooks, George G.

Brown, David W.

Brown, Dwight

Cappucino, Fred A.

Carnes, Paul N.

Cole, David H.

Cooper, Henry

Cope, J. Raymond

Cummins, John

Curry, Vernon L.

Doss, Robert M.

Doughty, Charles I.

Engel, Ron

Evans, John B.

Fay, Leon C.

Fritchman, Stephen H.

Fulghum, Robert L.

Gaede, Erwin A.

Gehr, Harmon M.

Gelsey, Rudolph C.

Gettier, Straughan

Gibson, Gordon

Gibson, Randall L.

Gilbert, Richard S.

Gilmartin, Aron S.

Graves, Steve

Greeley, Dana McLean

Greeley, W. Bradford

Gudmundson, V. Emil

Hadley, J. Harold

Harrington, Donald S.

Hawkes, Kenneth C.

Hayward, John F.

Hemstreet, Robert M.

Hild, Stewart E.

Hobart, Alfred W.

Hobart, James A.

Hoehler, Harry H.

Hohler, Robert

Hoffman, Clifton G.

Houff, William H.

Howard, Ernest L.

Howard, George C.

Isom, John B.

Jack, Homer A.

Jellis, Arthur B.

Johnson, David A.

Jones, Walter Royal Jr.

Kellison, Walter B.

Kent, Jack A.

Kimball, Robert C.

Kjelshus, Bjarne O.

Kolbjornsen, John M.

Krick, Gerald R.

Lane, Edwin A.

Leaming, Hugo P.

Leggitt, S. Hunter Jr.
Leonard, Richard D.
LeShane, Fred A.
Lewis, Ford
Lipp, Frederick
Loadman, Jack C.
Lion, F. Danford
Marshall, Kenneth K.
Matson, Howard G.
McKee, Lewis A.
McGinness, Mason F.
McGinty, Lawrence B.
McKeeman, Gordon B.
Mendelsohn, Jack
Mersky, Roy
Miller, Orloff W.
Morin, Roland E.
Morgan, John C.
Moors, William R.
Nash, Richard L.
Nelson, Carl J.
Nemser, Rudolph W.
Nerad, Joseph F.
Norsworthy, Richard J.
O'Brien, Robert J.
Olsen, Clark B.
Owen-Towle, Tom
Palmer, Robert C.
Papandrew, John
Peterman, Sidney A.
Pickett, Eugene
Raible, Christopher G.
Reeb, James

Schmidt, Harold B.
Schneiders, Joseph A.
Scholefield, Harry B.
Seiverts, Ed
Senghas, Robert E.
Shelley, Harold K.
Smith, Philip A.
Starr, Deane
Stephen, Charles S. Jr.
Stoll, James L.
Stutzman, Ralph
Sutherland, Malcolm R. Jr.
Taylor, John A.
Thaw, Arnold
Thompson, Donald A.
Thor, Harry
Ulrich, Carl
Vanstrom, Vester L.
Wassman, Donald L.
Webb, Theodore A.
Weir, William M.
Weller, Peter Jr.
Wells, Clarke D.
Wells, John M.
West, Robert Nelson
Weston, Richard
Westwood, Horace F.
Wheelwright, Farley W.
Whitney, George C.
Wilkinson, John
Wilmot, Arthur D.
Woodman, Richard M.

About the Photographs

All of the photographs in this book were taken by Ivan Massar. In the following piece, he gives his account of what it was like to be in Selma as a photojournalist:

When I learned in March 1965 that Martin Luther King would lead a march from Selma to Montgomery, I knew I had to be there. I was reminded of Gandhi's Salt March to the sea and Thoreau's opposition to the poll tax. As a photographer, I hoped to capture what was about to happen in Alabama.

I flew to Montgomery, where I was met by a young man who drove me to Selma (to avoid trouble from those who opposed King and his message). Viola Luizzo would be murdered later that week while driving that same shuttle.

I was given a room with a black family living across the street from Selma's Brown Chapel. The day before the march, I was told that I needed a press pass from Sheriff Jim Clark. Clark was in his office with some deputies, probably also preparing for the march. He asked what I wanted; I said that I needed a press pass for tomorrow's march. He asked, "Who you with?"

"Black Star," I replied. (This was the agency I worked through in New York.)

"*Black* Star!" exploded the Sheriff, "I never heard of *Black* Star."

I said, "It's the biggest and most respected picture agency in the country."

"Well," instructed the Sheriff, "I won't give you a press pass until I hear from the police chief in your hometown telling me you're okay." I left the sheriff's office, knowing it would be impossible to get a press pass before the next day's march to Montgomery.

The following morning I joined the long line of marchers, my camera tucked under my jacket until we were outside Selma. The next challenge after crossing the Edmund Pettus Bridge and leaving Sheriff Clark's domain was the photography itself. I was excited when we passed a large concrete cross inscribed with "Get Right With God," a perfect way to frame the distant dedicated marchers en route to Montgomery. The march was led by four men, two with American flags, one playing a fife, and a one-legged man on crutches, reminding me of the minutemen in my hometown of Concord. Dr. King and his wife Coretta, along with Ralph Abernathy, followed close behind, along with about three hundred volunteers. There was some apprehension about snipers along this desolate road, but the ever-present National Guard in trucks along the way, as well as helicopters overhead, made it seem a little less dangerous. Over the next three days we walked past signs with such messages as "White Citizens Council Welcomes you to Montgomery" and "Get U.S. out of the UN." Outside our encampment at night, soldiers stood to protect us from "night riders." There was no question there were those about who wished us harm.

We passed half a dozen young men standing by cars emblazoned with messages such as "Yankee trash go home," "Veterans of Oxford," and "Coon lovers go away." It seemed so sad. Black families appeared on their front porches to watch and to wave us on.

After several days' march, with fifty miles behind us, we arrived on the outskirts of Montgomery. We spent the last night before marching downtown to the capitol in a Catholic school gym with mats and sleeping bags on the floor. As we walked downtown in the morning I found a young man with "VOTE" written across his brown forehead with flour. Along the way I photographed a young black woman busily writing on her raincoat "50 miles in cold and rain—I have overcome." As we talked, she told me that she herself had not been involved in civil rights until a girlfriend took her to hear King speak. When her employer found out she'd been there, she was fired, and a new marcher was born.

As we marched past the Jefferson Davis Hotel, I saw a dozen white men in business suits watching from the balcony as a crowd of some 25,000 determined citizens moved toward the State House. At the steps to the Capitol we were greeted, not by Governor Wallace, but by a solid line of state police who blocked our way. The ceremony was held on these steps. Thousands of black and white demonstrators listened together to speeches by King and other dignitaries. The confederate flag flew atop the State House in the breeze. The Governor did not appear.

Ivan Massar was freelancing as a photographer for Black Star Publishing Company when he went to Selma in 1965. Massar has been a photojournalist and freelance photographer for more than fifty years. His pictures have appeared in many magazines, including Life, Look, National Geographic, *and* Fortune, *and his photographs of the events in Selma have been nominated for a 2001 Ozzie Award by* Folio Magazine.

Contributors' Notes

Gerry Bailey is president of the Unitarian Sunday School Society. In 1965 he attended a small suburban UU church in Rockville, MD, and was active in desegregation.

Charles Blackburn attends First Unitarian Church of Baltimore, Maryland. In 1965 he was minister of the UU Fellowship in Huntsville, Alabama.

Connie Burgess was executive director of the Unitarian Universalist Women's Federation in 1965. She died in 1995.

David H. Cole is an emeritus minister at West Shore Unitarian Universalist Church in Cleveland, Ohio. In 1965 he was the minister of Unitarian Church in Rockville, Maryland.

Helen Dick was involved with the South Acton Unitarian Universalist Church in Massachusetts as well as the Nashoba Association for Equal Rights in 1965. Her comments are excerpted from a letter written March 18, 1965.

Rudi Gelsey retired in 1999 as minister of the Unitarian Universalist Fellowship of New River Valley, Blacksburg, Virginia. In 1965 he was minister at the Universalist Church of the Restoration in Philadelphia, Pennsylvania.

Gordon Gibson is currently the minister of the Unitarian Universalist Fellowship of Elkhart, Indiana. In 1965 he was the minister of Theodore Parker Unitarian Church in West Roxbury,

Massachusetts. Some of his comments are excerpted from a sermon delivered on February 21, 1965.

W. Bradford Greeley is the Parish Minister at Main Line Unitarian Church in Devon, Pennsylvania. In 1965 he was a minister in associate fellowship with the Unitarian Universalist Association.

Robert Hemstreet is an emeritus minister at Unitarian Universalist Church in Flushing, New York. In 1965 he was the minister of First Unitarian Church of Hamilton, Ontario, Canada.

Robert Hohler was executive director of the Unitarian Universalist Laymen's League in 1965. His comments are excerpted from an article entitled "You Can't Jail Us All," published by the Laymen's League in 1965. He is now president of the Civil Rights Project, Inc.

Arthur Jellis is a retired Unitarian Universalist minister. In 1965 he was the minister of the First Parish in Concord, Massachusetts.

David A. Johnson is the minister of Shawnee Mission Unitarian Universalist Church in Overland Park, Kansas. In 1965 he was the minister of Unitarian Universalist Church in Bloomington, Indiana. His comments are excerpted from a sermon delivered on March 14, 1965.

Walter Royal Jones, Jr. is an emeritus minister at Foothills Unitarian Church in Fort Collins, Colorado. In 1965 he was the minister of Thomas Jefferson Memorial Unitarian Church in Charlottesville, Virginia, and chair of the UUA Commission on Religion and Race.

Edwin A. Lane is an emeritus minister at First Parish in Waltham, Massachusetts. In 1965 he was minister of the Unitarian Church of Southern New Jersey in Cherry Hill, New Jersey.

Hunter Leggitt is a retired Unitarian Universalist minister. In 1965 he was the minister of Beverly Unitarian Church in

Chicago, Illinois. His comments are excerpted from a sermon delivered March 21, 1965.

Richard D. Leonard is currently minister emeritus of the All Souls Unitarian Church in New York, where he has served with Dr. Forrester Church since 1979. He served as minister of education for the Community Church of New York from 1959 to 1968.

Ford Lewis was the minister of First Unitarian Society of Sacramento, California, in 1965. After his retirement in 1979, the congregation made him an emeritus minister. He died in 1998. His comments are excerpted from a sermon delivered on March 21, 1965.

Grace Linquist is currently a member of First Parish in Littleton, Massachusetts. In 1965 she was involved with the Nashoba Association for Equal Rights and a member of Arlington Street Church in Boston, Massachusetts.

Howard G. Matson died in 1993. In 1978 he retired from the Unitarian Universalist Ministry for Migrant Farm Workers, a specialized ministry of his own founding. In 1965, Rev. Matson was an associate minister at First Unitarian Church of San Francisco, California. His comments are excerpted from a sermon delivered on March 21, 1965.

Lawrence McGinty was an interim minister at First Parish Unitarian Universalist in Canton, Massachusetts, when he died in 1996. In 1965 he was the minister of First Unitarian Church in Birmingham, Alabama. His comments are excerpted from an article entitled "Selma: The Witness" in the Spring 1965 issue of *The Liberal Context.*

Elizabeth McMaster is currently an interim minister at the Unitarian Church in Los Alamos, New Mexico. In 1965 she was living in Atlanta, Georgia, with her husband and three children.

Orloff W. Miller is currently minister-at-large for European Unitarians and Universalists. In 1965 he was the director of the

Unitarian Universalist Association's Office of College Centers and staff advisor for Student Religious Liberals.

Irene K. Murdock lives in Sarasota, Florida, and attends the Unitarian Universalist Church in Sarasota. In 1965 she was the assistant to Dana Greeley, the president of the Unitarian Universalist Association.

Richard Norsworthy is a retired Unitarian Universalist minister. In 1965 he was the minister of the Third Universalist Church of Weymouth in North Weymouth, Massachusetts. His comments are excerpted from an article entitled "Selma: The Witness" in the Spring 1965 issue of *The Liberal Context*.

Tom Owen-Towle is co-minister of the First Unitarian Universalist Church of San Diego, California. In 1965 he was a student at San Francisco Theological Seminary.

Greg Street currently lives in Fairfax, Virginia, and is a budget officer for the Federal Aviation Administration. In 1965 he was a student at Groveton High School in Alexandria, Virginia.

Judy Hodson Street died in 1998. She was a long-time member of Mt. Vernon Unitarian Universalist Church in Alexandria, Virginia.

Ralph Stutzman is an emeritus minister at the Unitarian Universalist Congregation of Fairfax in Oakton, Virginia. In 1965 he was the minister of the Unitarian Fellowship of North Suffolk, Huntington, New York.

Arnold Thaw is a retired UU minister and emeritus member of the Gestalt Institute in Phoenix, Arizona. In 1965 he was the minister of Unitarian Congregation of South Peel, Port Credit, Ontario, Canada.

Theodore A. Webb is an emeritus minister at the Unitarian Universalist Society of Sacramento, California. In 1965 he was executive director of the Massachusetts Bay District of Unitarian Universalist Churches.

Clarke Dewey Wells is an emeritus minister at Lake Region Unitarian Universalist Fellowship in Lakeland, Florida. In 1965 he was the minister of St. John's Unitarian Church in Cincinnati, Ohio.

Una Joyce Williams attended the Unitarian Fellowship of North Suffolk, Huntington, New York, in 1965 and is still a member. She and her husband, Jack Williams, went to Selma as part of Social Workers for Civil Rights Action.

Acknowledgments

A great many people contributed to this book by sending heartfelt and vivid reminiscences of their time in Selma and Montgomery. This book was made possible not only by these gracious offerings but by the actions of all Unitarian Universalists who heeded the moral imperative of Selma.

A special thanks to Jack Mendelsohn and Judith Frediani, who contributed their time and hard work to collect these stories.